JOHN FORCE

THE STRAIGHT STORY OF
DRAG RACING'S 300–MPH SUPERSTAR

ERIK ARNESON

WITH PHOTOGRAPHY FROM **JON ASHER**

MOTORBOOKS

First published in 2006 by Motorbooks, an imprint of MBI Publishing Company, Galtier Plaza, Suite 200, 380 Jackson Street, St. Paul, MN 55101-3885 USA

Motorbooks titles are also available at discounts in bulk quantity for industrial or sales-promotional use. For details write to Special Sales Manager at MBI Publishing Company, Galtier Plaza, Suite 200, 380 Jackson Street, St. Paul, MN 55101-3885 USA.

ISBN-13: 978-0-7603-2221-5
ISBN-10: 0-7603-2221-X

Acquisitions Editor: Lee Klancher
Associate Editor: Leah Noel
Designer: Tom Heffron

On the frontispiece:
John Force is an American original, an icon in the world of drag racing and often called the best interview in sports. *Jeff Burke*

On the title page:
For John Force, the irresistible lure to drag racing came from watching the long, smoky burnouts performed by Southern California's best drag racers. Now, no one does it better than John. *Ron Lewis*

Printed in China

CONTENTS

DEDICATION

To Jo and C. P.—good friends who keep my life in perspective. You are missed.

ACKNOWLEDGMENTS

The challenge and responsibility of writing a book takes a great deal of support and encouragement, so I must, first and foremost, thank my wonderful family for all they do to support my efforts. My wife, Sandy, and my children, Eileen, Kyle, Jaret, and Dakota, are forever my inspiration. My parents, Jon and Meredith Arneson, my brothers, Brian and Jeff, and their families also provide encouragement, proofreading, and support. My in-laws, Judge Richard Linn and his wife, Patti, and my sister-in-law, Debbie, are always there to lend a hand and offer words of encouragement. Thank you all.

Specific to this project, I thank all of the people who took time out of their busy schedules to spend a few minutes with me on the phone or answering e-mails. Without your personal stories and direction, this book wouldn't have been possible.

I also offer my special appreciation to five good friends—David Harris, Mike Kerchner, Bill Osborn, Gregg Leary, and Susan Wade. David, you have always been my partner in drag racing, and I appreciate your knowledge of the sport and your unbending willingness to help me with any project. Mike, letting me spend some time with the *National Speed Sport News* archives over Christmas break helped me get this project started. I appreciate your willingness to help me whenever I've asked. Bill, thanks for knowing how much writing means to me and supporting my efforts to fit it into my life. And Susan, thanks for the extended phone call and the trust you showed by sharing your hard work. You have a vision of the sport and a style of writing unique to drag racing, and I very much appreciate how much you shared so openly.

GROWING UP FORCE

"I PLAYED QUARTERBACK IN HIGH SCHOOL AND NEVER WON A GAME. I WAS 0-29 IN THREE YEARS, BUT I NEVER GAVE UP. THAT'S WHY I NEVER GAVE UP ON RACING.
—JOHN FORCE, USA TODAY

John's famous gift of gab comes from his father Harold, a long-haul truck driver who always drew a crowd telling stories at truck stops across California. *Jon Asher*

As scalding hot water filled the bathtub, Betty Ruth Force stepped outside the family's silver 35-foot trailer home into the warm Southern California evening, hoping the cacophony of noises emanating from the small steel village would help her escape the screams she knew were inevitable. Her husband, Harold, worn by years on the road as a long-haul truck driver, locked the bathroom door so Betty could not come back in, trying in vain to conceal the tears running down his tired face as he dipped his youngest son into the painfully hot bath.

In the early 1950s, scientists still were several years from a safe vaccine for the poliomyelitis virus, a historically devastating illness that often paralyzed its victims. The Kenny treatment, named for the nurse who pioneered the approach, involved hot baths to relax the muscles. For John Harold Force, born May 4, 1949, and diagnosed with polio shortly after learning to walk, his father's extreme version of the nightly ritual blistered his legs and lasted for nearly a year.

Although no reference to the Kenny treatment calls for such a painful approach, the thinking might have been, "If hot water helps, hotter water helps more."

For John Force, today's consummate drag racer, that rationale apparently was absorbed through nurture and nature. If winning one race is good, winning them all is great. If winning one championship is good, winning more championships than any other quarter-miler in history is great.

Forever linked with classic leather-jacket movies like *Rebel Without a Cause* and *American Graffiti*, drag racing reached its highest profile in the mid-1970s with colorful drivers like Don "The Snake" Prudhomme, Shirley "Cha Cha" Muldowney, and "Big Daddy" Don Garlits making regular appearances on television's *Wide World of Sports*.

During that same time, Force was figuring out how to finance an escape from his blue-collar roots in hand-me-down hot rods with mix-and-match parts, bullshitting his way onto local tracks around Southern California.

Through hard work and hustle, camaraderie and con, and influenced by everyone from Elvis to Vince Lombardi to John F. Kennedy, Force became the best in the business, matching and surpassing all of the major records ever held in the sport.

THE GOSPEL ACCORDING TO JOHN

"YOU ASK MOST OF THE TOP DRIVERS AND THEY'LL TELL YOU THEY DREAMED OF WINNING THE WINSTON CHAMPIONSHIP WHEN THEY WERE GROWING UP. NOT ME. I USED TO WATCH THROUGH THE FENCES OF ORANGE COUNTY, AND MY DREAM WAS TO DO A BURNOUT LIKE 'THE SNAKE'."

— *LOS ANGELES TIMES*

Growing up in Southern California's car culture, John Force loved his hot rods. They served as sanctuaries—places of escape from a difficult life. *Jon Asher*

With more than a dozen Funny Car titles already attached to his legend, he isn't slowing down. After all, if winning 13 championships is great, winning 14 is better.

But despite his indisputable success as a driver, a businessman, and a P. T. Barnum-like showman on the NHRA circuit, John Force still lives in fear—an irreconcilable fear of losing it all and returning to his less-than-humble beginnings.

Very few things came easy to the Force family in the early years.

Driven into a nomadic lifestyle by Harold's job, the Force family often called the trailer court in Bell Gardens, California, home in the fall and winter. An industrial bedroom community among many others off what's now the 710 Freeway between Los Angeles and Long Beach, Bell Gardens was not the land of the rich and famous.

In the spring and summer, Harold loaded up the family and headed for work in the Northern California logging districts. On at least one occasion when work of any kind was hard to come by, the family leaned on Betty Ruth's Native American heritage and rented a small cabin and barn in Redwood Creek on the Hoopa Valley Indian Reservation, the largest Indian reservation in California.

Bisected by the Trinity River and surrounded by mountains timbered with pine, fir, and hardwoods, the 90,000-acre reservation housed seven saw mills in the 1950s and relied heavily on the logging industry as its economic foundation.

"We lived on the reservation, but we didn't live in teepees," Force told NHRA.com writer Rob Geiger. "It wasn't like that. It was just a small house, but it was home. . . . No one knew my

In high school, John wore a different kind of helmet and was cheered on by a football crowd as he played quarterback for the Bell Gardens Lancers. When the lingering effects from a childhood bout with polio ended his hopes of playing football beyond junior college, Force turned to racing. *Jon Asher*

mother was an Indian from Broken Arrow, Oklahoma. But back then, it sure helped because we were able to stay on the reservation, and it was right by where my dad was working."

"We were eating bologna sandwiches with no bologna," Force continued. "They were really just mustard sandwiches, and we had potatoes. Believe it or not, that's still my favorite food. I was asked that once by a reporter, and I answered, 'Bologna sandwiches without bologna, just the mustard.' You know why? Because when I sat down with Dad he would reach over and wipe a little mustard off my chin and tell me he loved me; that's all I needed."

For the Force family, the only thing constant was change.

"One year, we were in six or seven different schools," Force's brother, Walker, who is eight years older, told the *Los Angeles Times.* "You would think you'd get used to it, but I don't think a kid ever gets used to the terror you feel when you walk into a new school where everyone already knows everyone and you don't know anyone."

Force grew up sharing a bed with his parents or sleeping on a pull-out couch, while older brothers Walker, Tom, and Louie shared a bunk bed. Older sister Cindy was the only one with

Several NHRA officials went to series founder Wally Parks (right) trying to keep the inexperienced Force off the racetrack, out of fear for his safety and the safety of the other drivers. Here, John stands with Parks and Parks' wife, Barbara. *Ron Lewis*

her own bed. Space for clothes and personal items was limited at best.

"We were very crowded," Force told *Drag Racing Online* magazine. "On hot nights, one or two of us would sleep outside, under the awning."

By age seven, Force was prowling the sidelines at Bell Gardens High football games, serving as the ball boy for first-year graduate-assistant coach John McNichols and watching Walker play lineman for the perennially overmatched Lancers.

"Walker was a bright guy, an overachiever," recalls McNichols, who raced his Chevy as a teenager on the tracks of Pomona and Long Beach in the early 1950s. "Walker was a good student, a good athlete, a good guy, and I think he was a real good example to his younger brothers."

"They were all different. Louie's a good guy too," McNichols says with a chuckle. "We never got Louie into our football program—he was a bit of a loose cannon. One day, he was up on top of the gymnasium while we were starting football practice. He was doing varsity cheers from the top—this is probably a hundred feet in the air, and how he got up there, I'm still really not quite sure. But that was Louie. He wanted us to know he was there."

When John was 14, Harold spent time in a state hospital after suffering what Force described as a "nervous breakdown." "His life was not an easy one," Force explained. "It took its toll on him."

Force has never tried to hide tales of his father's dramatic temper, telling stories of being thrown from a pier in Newport Beach and having his surfboard sawed in half to "get his mind right."

John grew up the son of a long-haul truck driver, sleeping on a pull-out couch, sharing clothes with his brothers, and never staying many places long enough to call them home.
Ron Lewis

"I grew up a little wild," Force told *Drag Racing Online.* "My father said, 'You're uncontrollable. You got a whole idea about how life should be, and you're wrong.'" Despite Harold Force's volatile nature, John Force has great respect for his dad's values and work ethic. "I consider myself a race car driver. But my dad led a life like one," Force said in the same interview. "Back in the late 1930s and 1940s, there were very few truck drivers who had routes that ran the length of California. He was one of the few, maybe a half dozen, who had one of those routes. And that made him a hero.

"He'd pull right into a truck stop with a load of lumber, and people would say, 'All right, there he is. There's Willie.' My dad's nickname was Willie, and he was known at almost every truck stop. When I was younger, I'd tell people he hauled elephants for the Barnum & Bailey Circus, but in reality, he hauled hay. I was always BS-ing and conning, even as a little kid."

In high school, Force loved football, and his athleticism landed him the job of starting quarterback for his junior season.

"We weren't that successful," McNichols explains. "It was an extremely difficult league . . . but I don't think anyone worked any harder than John did."

Despite playing 27 games without a single victory during his high school career, Force showed up for every game expecting to win.

"John had a tremendous competitive spirit and a burning desire to play," McNichols says. "He loved to play, he loved to compete, and he had that ambition as a young guy. It was much harder to slow him down and calm him down than it was to fire him up," McNichols adds. "My challenge with John was to keep his feet on the ground, and his head right in the game and into what we were trying to accomplish rather than just letting him run—because he would have been real happy to call all the plays himself and do whatever he wanted."

"WE'RE GOING TO MAKE A MOVIE ABOUT ME. MY BROTHER WANTS TO CALL IT 'FORCE GUMP.' STARTS OUT WITH ME AS A LITTLE KID WITH POLIO. I WANT KURT RUSSELL TO PLAY ME."

– JOHN FORCE, *LOS ANGELES TIMES*

Early in the first game of his senior season, Force became so excited that he was over-throwing receivers and making a lot of mistakes. Eventually, McNichols called a timeout.

"John came over to the sidelines, and I kept telling him, 'You gotta calm down, you gotta calm down,'" McNichols says. "He said, 'It's okay coach, I'm calmed down now, I'm calmed down now.' He was so wired up, even at that point, that he knew what he had to do, but doing it was tough. I don't think I will ever forget that.

"John loved to play, he loved the sport," McNichols adds. "He didn't play any other sports that I can remember. He didn't do much else athletically. Football, his car, and his girlfriend—and probably in that order—were his main interests."

"I had this '54 Chevy," Force told *Drag Racing Online*. "It was a six-cylinder and wasn't the bitchinest car there by any means, but it was mine, and I was proud of it. I had a car stereo in it and everything. The cars I dreamed of having were the Chevy Malibu Super Sports or the Corvettes. I'd love to have had one of those, but this had to do until I could get one."

"I faked it a lot with this car. It was a four-door, but I took off the two rear-door handles and buffed it so it would look like a two-door," Force added. "I put Mickey Thompson mag wheels in the front and big old slicks in the back, and uncorked the motor. I'd go rumbling through the place, and a guy came up to me and wanted me to open the hood. They all wanted you to open the hood and see what was underneath, and I said, 'Pull out your money and let's race, and see what I've got.' It's a good thing most of them never took me up on it because the combination of that little motor and big tires would've got me killed. I always was faking it."

The car with the cracked windshield and tuck-and-roll upholstery from Tijuana was also a four-wheel sanctuary. For any teenager, especially in Southern California in the 1960s, your car was an integral part of your identity—an extension of your personality. For Force, it was even more so.

"I'd go out and sleep in it at nights just because there was more room in it," Force continued. "I could put my stuff in it, and it was like my own little place. I'd drive it around and stay out late night and became a street kid. Then I'd come home late at night, put on that car stereo, and look out that front window and dream of the day I'd get out of Bell Gardens and have a place of my own."

"I used to stay in the parking lot of Taco Bell until midnight, do my homework or just hang out," Force told the *Los Angeles Times.* "The car became a way of life. You didn't want to go home until you were ready to get into bed."

"I also [went there] when I didn't feel like staying home at the trailer, and that was a lot," Force told Chris Martin, of *Drag Racing Online.* "I'd come here at night and tell stories and entertain my friends, and if they had a good time, they'd buy me dinner. I wasn't poor, but a free meal is a free meal. All kinds of things happened to me here."

Down the road was the community of Downey and Harvey's Broiler, an area landmark that was one of the last mammoth drive-in restaurants built in Southern California. On any given night in the early 1960s, the popular spot for teenagers and their cars employed nearly 100 people full time. Built on a two-acre lot just off a busy highway, Harvey's Broiler welcomed up to 1,000 cars on a weekend night, with cars lined up a block away for their turn to cruise through the crowd. Ironically, after going through another set of owners, Harvey's is now part of an expansive car dealership lot. Rows and rows of machines only separated by color and label now sit lifeless on the same turf that once roared with activity and countless flavors of teenage behavior in an area known as Oklahoma by the Sea.

Writer Tom Wolfe, in his short story "The Hair Boys," described a night of cruising at Harvey's Broiler in the early 1960s this way:

> Every Friday night at Harvey's, starting about 9:30 p.m., kids from all over the Los Angeles teenage netherworld, from West Los Angeles, Bell, Maywood, Hollywood, Gardena, San Pedro, white Watts, San Gabriel, even Santa Ana, Santa Monica, Covina—they all drive to Harvey's Drive-in in their cruising cars. The real reason they come is simply to promenade, or, in the parlance of Harvey's Drive-in, to cruise. They cruise around in their cars in Harvey's huge parking lot, boys and girls, showing each other the latest in fashions in cars, hairdos [male and female], and clothes.

Harvey's was about one thing: showing off. And nobody showed off better than John Force, even if it was just another way to escape.

"I loved cars because they could take you away from the pain," he told Susan Wade for a story in *Performance Trends* magazine. "It's hard to explain, the pain of just growing up in poverty." Force seems to vacillate some on whether he was poor himself, as if it's not a badge anyone wants to wear. He viewed himself as growing up with little, and that background shaped his personality and his desire.

After high school, Force took his love of football to East Los Angeles Community College, where his quarterbacking skills reached their limit despite his eagerness to play.

Always on the move, John didn't have a stable childhood. Moving and changing schools were commonplace for John, his brothers, and sister, as their father's nomadic job uprooted the family on a regular basis.
Carol Johnson

John Force, drag racing's greatest ambassador for the last decade, entertains crowds, keeps sponsors happy, and wins more races than anyone else. *Jon Asher*

John's secret to his early success—match racing. Long after many of the biggest names in the sport left the match-racing circuit, John and his team kept at it, leaving them better prepared for changes in weather and track conditions at national events. _Jeff Burk_

"In those days, they had a good football program, and Force was as good a quarterback as they had," McNichols says. "Every high school player isn't a college football player, but Force's competitive fires caught the coaches' attention."

Force's childhood bout with polio, however, left him with minor muscle atrophy and one leg slightly shorter than the other, limiting his running ability and ending his college gridiron career not long after it started.

But as one door closed, John Force became determined to find another. Little did anyone know that his love of cars and his knack for telling stories would offer passage to a world of fame and fortune.

FAKE IT 'TIL YOU MAKE IT

"IT AIN'T LIKE I WAS A BILLIONAIRE THAT WALKED IN HERE AND SAID, 'I'M HOWARD HUGHES AND I WANT TO RACE.' I HAD NOTHIN'–FLAT NOTHIN.'"

– JOHN FORCE, MUSTANG MAGAZINE

John had no business behind the wheel of a Funny Car early in his career, but he was determined to play on the same playground with guys like Don "The Snake" Prudhomme and Tom "The Mongoose" McEwen. *Jeff Burk*

John's first choice of career was the same as his father's—he decided to become a truck driver shortly after starting his own family (he married girlfriend Lana Bonee at 19 and became a father when daughter Adria was born on June 4, 1969, shortly after his 20th birthday).

But neither his new job nor his new responsibilities as a husband and father kept him from hanging out at the local racetracks on Saturday nights and gravitating toward the gypsy lifestyle that came so natural to him.

John often took his mother's Buick to Lions Drag Strip, a track built in 1955 by Mickey Thompson on an unused railroad switching yard and funded, in part, by local Lions Club International chapters in an effort to curb illegal street racing in Long Beach and neighboring communities. At Lions, seeing 64 Funny Cars under the lights on a Saturday night was magical, and John became hooked on life at the drag strip, going through a variety of low-dollar, quarter-mile hot rods.

Getting John even closer to the action were his cousins, Gene Beaver and Dave Condit. They and their families were regulars on the local drag racing circuit with the popular cars, like the *LA Hooker*, entered in Coca-Cola Cavalcade of Stars Funny Car events. The barnstorming series and its member drivers traveled to any track willing to pay for a show.

"Growing up, I drove all kinds of cars," John told *Drag Racing Online*. "But my first trophy car was a white '61 Corvette, the one with the double headlights and the little long glass in the back . . . . I remember I went out there and won my class with a shoe polish number on my window."

Long before he ever won a race, John mastered his trademark burnout. A year later, after campaigning the *Brute Force* car (pictured here), Force entered his first NHRA national event. *Jon Asher*

"YOU CAN'T WIN EVERY RACE. YOU LEARN HOW TO LOSE, [AND] YOU'LL BE A REAL WINNER. I HAD TEN YEARS OF LOSING, EVERY WEEK. I NEVER CAME HERE TO WIN. I CAME HERE BECAUSE I LOVED IT."

—MUSTANG MAGAZINE

John's first "professional car" was an Albertson's Olds look-alike he bought for $150.

"We took it to Lions, and I was out there with Don Prudhomme and Tom McEwen, but they didn't even know who I was—or care. We made only one run because we forgot clearance for the bearings, and at eight hundred feet, it was on fire. . . . In the beginning, I couldn't even see the stands. I said, 'Oh my God, am I going to die out here?' The highlight of that day wasn't the fire, though. It was my brother Louie standing on the back of the truck cheering because the car had left the starting line for the first time," he said.

When John got started out in racing, his parents helped financially when they could. Louie was the crew, and favors from friends kept Force going back for more.

"I've watched John for more than twenty years," John McNichols says. "His brother used to tow his car behind a pickup truck to a body shop in Bell Gardens to a guy John went to school with named Jim Allen. Jim worked at the body shop for his father-in-law, and he painted John's cars for free because if he didn't, they wouldn't get painted—and John banged them up."

Early on, John Force just wanted a little bit of what he had watched through the fences as a kid. He wanted to do big, smoky burnouts and hear the roar of the crowd. He wanted to be a star but never fancied himself a future world champion of anything. He simply enjoyed the show and wanted to be a part of it.

Rolling into his early twenties, John Force was a truck driving husband and young father still looking for his place in the world. All he really knew was that he couldn't sit still. He had to keep moving. The adventure was just beginning.

After a short-lived campaign in a fuel-altered—a shorter wheel-base ride with an altered body—John Force's first Funny Car was a Mustang Mach I rear-engine sidewinder built by Jack Chrisman in the early 1970s.

"It was pretty evil handling," Force told *Car Craft*. "Your feet were out in front like an Indy car, and you could get into trouble before you knew it. It never ran quicker than seven seconds."

In 1978, with small-change sponsor money from Leo's Stereo, Force
switched from a Chevy Monza to a Corvette. In 1979, John entered six
NHRA national events. *Jon Asher*

That ride quickly came to an end, however, when the sideways-mounted engine threw a
chain as Force's car tried to get off the line at Lions Drag Strip. Though it certainly wasn't the first
time the sidewinder had fallen apart, this particular time, as Force tells it, the chain nearly
wrapped around the neck of longtime starter and drag racer Larry Sutton.

"He was the worst driver in the history of sport," Sutton says about Force. "I, on numerous
occasions, went to the NHRA [National Hot Rod Association] to get him banned because I was
afraid he'd kill himself. He hit everything but the tower. The NHRA would give him notice that he
was on probation, and then he would go out and get by that period, and I'd have to go back and
say, 'Hey guys, we've gotta do something.' He was an accident waiting to happen, but he was
going to race no matter what. He would beg and borrow to be able to make another lap—he
was a scrounger, but one thing about John, he never quit. As much shit as I and everyone else
gave him, he still would come back. He was just trying to go out and run."

At one point, John decided racing wasn't going to work out, so he attempted to join his
brother Walker in law enforcement. That didn't work out either, as John regularly claims to have
"failed the ink blot test."

"Walker told me to tell the truth," Force explained to the *Los Angeles Times*. "All I saw was
snakes and spiders and [stuff], and that's what I told 'em. So, they failed me."

Finally, in 1974, John got the break he needed.

While living with Walker, using money cobbled together from his $1,200 tax return and cash earned from selling an electric organ he says his mother-in-law won on the TV game show *Let's Make a Deal*, John purchased a broken Vega Funny Car from his cousin, Gene Beaver. That same year, Australian promoters working with *Hot Rod* magazine editor Ray Brock were looking to fill a touring race ticket. When U.S. racers "Jungle" Jim Liberman and Ed McCulloch backed out of the planned five-race series, Beaver secured a spot for the inexperienced Force. To give the Australians the impression they were getting a real racer, John Force sent over a picture of his car lined up next to Dale Pulde in the Mickey Thompson Pontiac at Orange County International Raceway in Irvine, California. The fact that the two cars were standing still and had never raced each other didn't seem to make much of a difference.

On his way to Australia, John struck up a conversation at the Honolulu airport with veteran racer Gary Densham, a California high school auto shop teacher who raced the *Teacher's Pet* Funny Car. Densham was bound for the same series.

The *Hot 'n' Juicy* Wendy's Corvette was known around the circuit as a leaker—a poorly tuned car that routinely left oil and parts on the track. Using mix-and-match parts and an inexperienced crew, John and his friends had to be creative just to get into local drag racing events.
Jon Asher

John's competitive spirit is unparalleled in drag racing, a trait that came through even before he sat in his first race car. Despite quarterbacking his high school through several seasons of winless football, his coach said, "He loved to play. He loved to compete."
Ron Lewis

Gary Densham, a shop teacher at Gahr High School in Cerritos, California, for more than 30 years, campaigned the *Teacher's Pet* Funny Car for much of his drag racing career. Densham first crossed paths with John Force en route to a Funny Car barnstorming trip to Australia. *Steve Reyes*

"I had no clue who John Force was," Densham told NHRA.com. "He had just bought his Funny Car. He was all decked out in jackets with Truckmaster sponsorship, and, even though we had no idea who he was, we thought we were in real trouble, that we were going to get our butts kicked. It was just me and a couple of buddies, and he looked like he had a whole professional team. He walked the walk and talked the talk."

It didn't take long, however, for John Force to be unmasked. At the group's first event at Surfer's Paradise, John's absolute incompetence came shining through.

"The first time he rolled through the water, he hit the gas and the engine just about died," Densham said in one interview. "He backed up to try it again and laid down a burnout that impressed me—one that would have put Jungle Jim to shame. The only problem is that about one hundred feet down the track I saw fire billowing out from under the car. He'd thrown all the rods out."

Realizing Force and his team of misfits didn't know much about servicing a broken race engine, Densham helped the young team get things back together. "One of them didn't know much more than how to operate a rag," Densham says.

Without a competitor's license, John Force continued destroying parts, surprising himself and others with an accidental run of 200 hundred miles per hour at one point, setting the Australian national speed record. But most runs weren't nearly as spectacular, and Densham continued helping him put the car back together again and again.

"I blew the engine, the car caught on fire and stopped in a cow pasture," Force told the *Las Vegas Review-Journal*. "I thought it was the end of my career. Me and Gary went to a junkyard to get the rear end out of a Ford Bronco, and Gary put my car back together, and we finished the tour in Australia."

Gary Densham befriended John Force early in Force's career, offering invaluable mechanical assistance when Force and his crew didn't really know how to get down the drag strip. Nearly 30 years later, Force repaid the debt, adding Densham to his stable of drivers. *Ron Lewis*

At the final event at Surfer's Paradise, the tandem ran out of fixes. "We went back to Surfer's Paradise for the final event, and I thought we were both going to get killed," Densham told NHRA.com. "At this final event, instead of John and I racing one another, they wanted us to race one of their racers. You can imagine eighteen thousand angry, drunken fans wanting to see more racing and, well, not seeing much actual racing.

"John was supposed to race Jim Read, and I was supposed to run Bobby Dunn. The place was packed. On the first run, John breaks the rear end again just off the line, and Read shells all of the rods out ten feet off the starting line. I'm figuring that I really need to step it up for the crowd, so I decide that I'm going to put down a quarter-mile burnout. I break the blower belt. Dunn shuts off and runs a twelve-second pass. The crowd is just getting madder and madder, and John is off hiding somewhere because he can't fix his car."

On the next run, Densham tried to get his car up and running again, but it just kept shaking and vibrating. It turned out that the pilot bearing had fallen out of the flywheel, so Densham had to shut the car off again. "By now, the Aussies *really* want to kill me. They're yelling, 'Go home, Yankee' and stuff like that, and it was just terrible," he said.

"On the last run, I do the burnout, and the next thing I know, my car is on fire. Because we hadn't had time to work on the car, we had some blow-by and it just pushed the gaskets out

Standing on a stage with a "Wally"—an NHRA national event win trophy named for series founder Wally Parks and first handed out to winners in 1969—seemed worlds away as John struggled throughout the 1980s to finance his fledgling career. *Jeff Burk*

from under the valve covers. . . . Luckily, the fire blew out instead of getting worse, and I set low E.T. [elapsed time] and top speed. All of a sudden, it was OK again."

As the adventure came to a close, Densham's airport impression of Force had changed dramatically. "Based on what I'd seen, I figured John was going to kill himself; it was that simple," Densham told NHRA.com. "I figured he had no chance of ever making it."

"It was the first time I'd been out of California, the first time I'd been on an airplane, and the first time I'd driven a Funny Car," Force said in a press release. "We really didn't know what we were doing, but [Densham] was over there and kind of got us through it all and got me back home."

When he returned home with the money earned in Australia, *Brute Force* was in business as a full-time Funny Car driver, and Densham continued to offer John help when their paths crossed at the track.

Off track, John's life on the road wasn't mixing well with his marriage. He eventually split with Lana, and despite the team's little sponsor money from local companies like Truckmasters, Sterling Transit, and Don Steves (a local Chevy dealer who gave John a gas credit card), John's brother Walker wasn't convinced his kid brother was doing the right thing.

A chance run-in with Jolly Rancher president Bob Harmsen led to sponsorship, gas, and shop assistance from the candy giant, while the Mountain Dew money came from a local California bottler. *Jon Asher*

Working with accomplished crew chiefs like Bill Schultz and Henry Velasco early in his career, John headed into the early 1980s with a little more experience, but had yet to find the big-dollar sponsor that would allow his team to consistently battle for wins. *Jon Asher*

"I kept telling him, 'You are determined to kill yourself. You are going to die in this junk,'" Walker said in an interview with *Performance Trends*. "[The car] was held together with bailing wire and duct tape. He was just crazy, a daredevil. I honestly didn't think he was going to make it. He doesn't get heart attacks. He gives heart attacks. But one characteristic that John has that makes him a winner is that he never, ever, ever gives up. You can knock him down, whip him, stomp on him, but the next day, he'll be knocking on your door."

In 1978, with a little sponsor money from Yamaha of Buena Park and Leo's Stereo, Force entered his first NHRA Funny Car national event with a Chevy Monza. A year later, he made six national events, making it to a pair of final rounds in his Wendy's-sponsored Corvette and finished eighth in points.

Steve Querico, a track and race promoter who met John Force through a longstanding friendship with Gene Beaver, took on the task of promoting the novice racer. Without a major sponsor and with even less skill as a driver, John placed the fate of his furture, in large part, on Querico's creativity.

"He was still driving a truck for Sterling Transit, and his race shop was a bay at a local gas station in Yorba Linda—we called him The Shah of Yorba Linda," Querico says. "We certainly had our work cut out for us."

"John's home track was Orange County, but they didn't even want him there," adds Querico, who spent his pre-teen years hawking race magazines at local drag strips. "We made a deal with a local alternative rock radio station, KROQ, putting their decals on John's car and setting up displays around town. In return, KROQ gave us twenty-five thousand dollars in radio airtime. So, when Charlie Allen, known as 'Cheap Charlie' at the time, was only offering fifteen

John rarely registered on the racing radar early in his career. Drag racing legend Don "The Snake" Prudhomme says he usually paid more attention to the guys that did their own work on the car and John wasn't doing that. *Jon Asher*

hundred dollars as an appearance fee, we were able to get three thousand dollars for John by trading Charlie five thousand dollars in airtime to promote his events."

The pair would hustle everywhere from street corners to trade shows, trying to find any dollar available.

"I tried to get John booked at a car show, but the promoter said there was no money in the budget to pay us," Querico says. "I offered to bring John's car in for free, if he could give us a twenty-by-twenty-foot area next to the car. He agreed, and we made a call to a local video game company. This was around the time when Pac-Man was a big deal, so we had a bunch of video games set up next to John's car. At the end of the day, we made about twenty-five hundred dollars—our cut from the video game company. If we would have set up the car for just an appearance fee, it might have only earned us a few hundred dollars."

No matter how much money was involved, Force made sure everyone got their dollar's worth.

"He was working hard for his sponsors even back then," says Joe Sherk, a former motorsports reporter with the *Seattle Post-Intelligencer*. "I remember the Seafair Funny Car Championships, an all-day event back in 1979 that was part rock concert, part sixty-four-car drag race. In the middle of the day, John and his team packed up their car, left the track, did an appearance at a local Wendy's, and then brought everything back and raced."

In fact, while he was racing with Wendy's as his principal sponsor, Force even took a gig that required that he put on the red pigtails and outfit worn by the hamburger chain's namesake. "The girl that was supposed to do it didn't show," he once said, "and they were paying fifty dollars, so I said I'd do it. That'd buy a lot of bologna sandwiches."

"John intentionally made sponsor deals look larger than they really were," Querico says. "With Wendy's, he basically got cheeseburgers and display money. With Mountain Dew, it was only a deal with a local Pepsi distributor, not with the parent company. He made a deal that might have been worth two thousand a month look like a five hundred thousand dollar sponsorship. His goal was to eventually turn one of these small deals into a big one."

Getting sponsor money was one thing. Getting into races was another.

"It was never easy in the early days," Querico adds. "John was a bit of a joke. He was known as a leaker—a term given to ill-prepared cars that left a lot of junk on the track—so getting him booked into races was not a simple task. One time, a promoter offered us fifteen hundred dollars

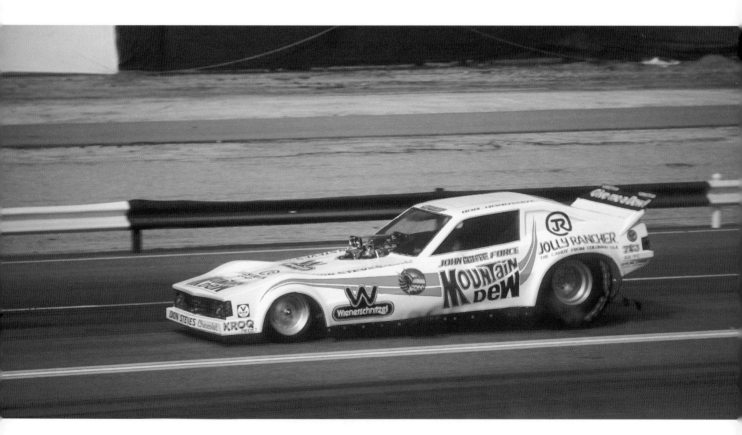

John made deals with alternative rock radio station KROQ (front quarterpanel) by trading car appearances for radio air time. He'd then trade the air time to promoters to be able to race in their events.
Ron Lewis

As John improved on the track, his endless effort to add sponsors began paying off. But adding new names was nothing compared to how long he kept old ones. *Jolly Rancher* **stayed with John for nearly 10 years.** *Ron Lewis*

just because he wanted to fill his sixty-four-car field. John was so mad at me. He said, 'Steve, I'm worth more than fifteen hundred,' and we started to scuffle right there in the middle of his house. Next thing you know, we'd busted right through a screen door."

Bill Schultz, a top-notch tuner called in on occasion when Force could afford him, recalls the first time the Wendy's executives came to the track. "They were surprised by how big the operation was," Schultz says. "I couldn't believe that these people had given John money with no idea what he had. But John had a way of finding at least one guy at a company and making him a buddy. If he thought he needed to be the guy at the party that got drunk and threw lawn furniture into the pool, he'd do it. He has a natural ability to make people feel relaxed and trust him."

Those skills came into play almost daily. On one occasion, Force asked Schultz to take the clutch can, the transmission, and the clutch out of the race car. They loaded it into Force's truck and he left the track for a few hours, bringing it back for the guys to re-install.

"Evidently, John had sold a second set of the same equipment that he had borrowed from someone," Schultz says. "He took the parts out of the race car and drove them over to the guy and said, 'See, I still have your parts.' But, in reality, those parts had been sold to keep John moving down the road."

Things didn't always work so smoothly, however, as John was constantly looking over his shoulder, spending at least one night camped in a tree in his front yard.

"He sat up there all night with a shotgun," Schultz says. "He said he owed somebody some money. You never know if those stories are true, but he certainly did things that made them believable."

While constantly on the prowl for money and parts, John and his makeshift crew—made up of family and old truck driving buddies—tried to learn all they could about running a race team. Despite some guidance from his racing cousins, John was basically starting from scratch, bringing in paid help only when he could afford it—or when he couldn't afford not to.

"John thought tuning a Funny Car was like getting a tune-up at your local gas station," Schultz says. "I'd come in and work for one or two races and he'd say he didn't have money to keep me around. They'd run that setup for two or three months, until they had it all screwed up, and then they'd bring me back in again.

"John didn't know anything about the mechanics of the car. I'd be working on something and he'd be talking to a fan, and the fan would ask, 'Were you running too lean?' John didn't have any idea, so he'd come over and act like that might have been the problem, so I had to show him it wasn't. He was taking tune-up suggestions from the people hanging around his pits."

John had no mechanical knowledge of the race car early in his career. Crew chiefs would give him busy work just to keep him away from the car. He was running on instinct and natural athletic ability. *Ron Lewis*

On-again, off-again crew chief Bill Schultz once said this about John: "There is something mythical about the guy." *Ron Lewis*

Without the money to pay Schultz, or anyone else, to be a full-time crew chief, Force and his buddies tried their best to learn as much as they could simply by watching.

"When I'd work on the car, John and Bob Fisher would run around writing things down, recording valve sizes and things like that," Schultz says. "But in those days, the craftsmanship on the parts was not as consistent as it is today, and John's team was using a lot of used and mismatched parts, so none of what they were writing down really meant anything."

Force's lack of mechanical knowledge also made for some adventures on the racetrack. "One of the first times I worked with John, we were in Denver," Schultz says. "John asked me how far I wanted him to drive it to set the transmission, and I told him about two hundred or three hundred feet. He asked how far that was, so we walked it off, and there was an outhouse off to the side that was about two hundred feet down the track, so I told him to drive it to the outhouse. The next night, we were doing the same thing, and he drove the car a thousand feet down the track before shifting gears—smoke and oil flying out all over the place. I asked him, 'Why the hell did you do that?' Someone had moved the outhouse farther down the track, and John had driven it to the outhouse as he was told. He knew nothing about cars."

Force, though, kept finding just enough money to keep learning, and each run down the track gave him a little more experience and a little more knowledge. In John's first final-round appearance, the 1979 Cajun Nationals at State Capitol Dragway just outside of Baton Rouge, Louisiana, his hot rod broke, and Kenny Bernstein went on to collect his first career victory.

"I made a career of letting other guys get their first win against me," Force told the *Los Angeles Times.* "Kenny Bernstein, Raymond Beadle, John Lombardo, Tim Grose, John Collins all got their first win against me, and Mark Oswald got his first Funny Car win against me."

Despite showing flashes of competitiveness—or simple blind luck—the giants of the sport still were not ready to welcome John Force into the upper echelon of their full-throttle fraternity.

"I didn't really pay much attention to John in those days," Don Prudhomme says. "He was one of the first guys out there with an eighteen-wheeler, so I noticed that, but I didn't recognize them as a team to be concerned with. I usually paid more attention to the guys that did their own work on the car, and John wasn't doing that.

"Back then, it was The Snake [Prudhomme], The Mongoose [Tom McEwen], [Don] Garlits, and others," Prudhomme adds. "John was just one of the *others*. We beat them quite regularly."

Force, though, continued to get better while no one was looking, sometimes through effort and sometimes by accident.

John's difficult childhood taught him never to give up. His brother Walker once said the following about John's perseverance: "You can knock him down, whip him, stomp on him, but the next day, he'll be knocking on your door." *Jon Asher*

From day one, John gave every sponsor its money's worth. Whether it was dressing up in a Wendy's costume, setting up a display for a local radio station, or serving as company pitchman, he did whatever it took to keep racing. *Jeff Burk*

"When tire shake started becoming an issue, John was credited with being able to flop the pedal and get back into the gas, but it didn't start as something he planned, understood, or knew anything about," Schultz says. "I was watching him on a run, and at about a hundred feet, his flames went out just briefly. I asked him about it when he got back, and he said he didn't do anything."

"I called 'Uncle Beavs' [Force's cousin and mentor, Gene Beaver] over and told him what I saw," Schultz adds. "He walked away with John and had to convince him he was lifting off the throttle. The throttle slap he is so well known for was simply a natural reaction—his body did it without his mind knowing why. He is a relatively natural athlete, and this time, his lack of mechanical knowledge actually helped him. While a lot of drivers are trying to figure out what the car is doing, John is just getting it from point A to point B. He had to know it by feel because he didn't know it mechanically. There is something mythical about the guy."

So, without really knowing what he was doing, Force kept looking for money and kept getting better a quarter mile at a time. "I had to quit for a while because I ran out of money," Force said in a press release. "I tapped my mom and dad out, and they ran their credit cards up. I remember running out of diesel fuel and having to negotiate with local companies to get money to go on to the next race. There was always something like that going on.

"One time, I ran out of money in Houston and called my dad to tell him I was broke. He said we're all broke, but there was a guy at a track in Houston that would pay me forty-five hundred dollars to come out and match race because Prudhomme had to cancel. I went there, and that gave me the opportunity to continue on."

John admits that many time he got calls to race because promoters knew how much fans loved seeing smoky burnouts, and he could always provide that. He also loved to talk with fans,

It took years for John's ability and budget to reach a competitive level. In the beginning, the program ran on little more than desire. *Jon Asher*

something more successful drivers didn't always like to do. "Then that became almost as good as me winning races," he said.

John's wheeling and dealing talents always came in handy during these lean times. At one point, in fact, after sitting at a truck stop in Denver, out of fuel and with no money for diesel, he realized he was just down the road from the Jolly Rancher candy company. Hoping for little more than trading a tank of fuel for a logo on the side of the race car, John hooked up with the company's president, Bob Harmsen. Fast-talking Force and the candy man became instant friends, with Jolly Rancher not only signing on as a sponsor but also giving Force and his crew access to the company's fiberglass works for emergency repairs.

"In the early days, John would gas up his oversized tanks at Sterling Transit, where he had driven trucks, and head for Colorado, where he would refill at Jolly Rancher's trucking facility," Querico says. "It was the only way he could make it to events in Florida. He couldn't have made it without these friendships."

With just enough money to get in trouble, John Force was looking to upgrade his equipment for the 1981 season. His Corvette—painted in the oddly shaded greens and golds of Pepsi's Mountain Dew brand, with the Jolly Rancher signature circled "R" on the rear quarterpanel and the Sterling Transit lettering on the front quarterpanel—needed more power if he had any hopes of ever winning an NHRA national event.

So, at the end of the season, John approached longtime racer Henry Velasco. From nearby Downey, Velasco was a partner and crew chief on several race teams, including Dunn, Merritt, and Velasco with a supercharged small-block Chevy-powered Fiat.

If you put a camera at one end of the track and a trophy at the other, it would create an interesting dilemma for John Force. *Jon Asher*

"Force was a wild man," recalls Jim Dunn's son, Mike, who spent many of his teenage years working with and for Velasco at Reath Automotive and then Velasco Crankshaft Service. "I didn't know John personally back then, but they worked on the car at Henry's shop, and I remember seeing him at the track. He'd do fourteen little dry hops before he did his burnout, and eighteen more it seemed like before he made the run. He was just out of control."

In 1980, Velasco campaigned a Top Fuel ride known as *The Good, Bad & Ugly*. The car was piloted by famed chassis builder Dave Uyehara, but Velasco was making plans to retire the ride at the end of the 1980 season. Enter John Force.

"I remember we crashed our car at Ontario [California] in the last race of the year," Velasco says. "John came to me over the winter . . . and he asked about putting my motors in his Funny

Car, with the stipulation that at the end of the year, he would buy all of my equipment—motors, transmissions, clutch parts—everything. And you know John: He can talk you into anything.

"I'll never forget, we were sitting there together that night, and John came out and said he was going to be the world champion one day. I laughed out loud. Even Laurie [John's second wife] laughed. But he was dead serious."

With Velasco's motors powering Force's machine, Velasco serving as crew chief, and Force's regular misfit crew consisting of little more than his brother Louie and friend Bob Fisher, the team showed up for the season opener at Pomona and qualified an impressive second behind Raymond Beadle. At the next race, the car set a national speed record at just over 246 miles per hour, before it was broken the same day by Prudhomme's 247 miles per hour.

"That was our brief moment in the sun," Velasco says with a chuckle. But the early success for the pairing didn't last long, as the team ran out of enough money to keep the car performing up to its potential.

"The blower was going away, and we didn't have the money to replace it, so we just tried to keep patching it together," Velasco says. "In an effort to get more boost, we were burning up pistons.

"We caught fire at a match race in Sacramento. We spent all night working on it and patching it back together, so we could get to a race in Denver. At Denver, we kept burning the pistons, and we caught on fire again. John went into a tantrum and said I was trying to kill him. We started wrestling and rolling around in the dirt. No punches were thrown, but there was a lot of screaming and hollering. I threatened to quit, but again, John talked me into staying."

While Velasco tried to figure out how to keep Force on the racetrack and away from the flames, Querico kept promoting. His sister told him about a new band that was playing clubs like The Whiskey Bar and The Troubadour. The band didn't have a manager, but it was starting to develop a loyal local following.

"I booked them at the Santa Monica Civic Auditorium," Querico recalls. "We got Elvira to be the emcee, and we put John's Corvette up on the stage. We sold the place out. That little-known band with no management was Mötley Crüe. They asked me to be their manager, but I wanted to be a promoter—biggest mistake of my life."

Motley Crue frontman Vince Neil remembers the evening well.

"I think we had two of his cars on stage," Neil says. "It was called 'Live Evil' or something like that, but it was pretty cool because we tried to have a Miss Nude contest before the Funny Cars came out . . . the cool thing was starting up the Funny Cars on stage as our intro."

"Those guys loved drag racing," Querico adds. "Their song *Kickstart My Heart*, where the guitar opening sounds like cars shifting gears down the strip, includes the lyrics, 'When I get high, I get high on speed. Top Fuel Funny Car's a drug for me.' That is about John's car."

At the end of the 1981 season, Jolly Rancher pressured Force to find a new crew chief, and Velasco was let go. Force, however, made good on his promise and bought all of Velasco's equipment. A short time later when Bill Schultz installed a new blower on Force's car, the hot rod perked back up to its early season performance levels.

"I can honestly say that year included some of the most fun in my entire drag racing career," Velasco says. "John had an amazing ability to promote himself. He could talk anybody into anything and he could make things happen for the least amount of money. He certainly had the fire."

JOHN FORCE, MEET AUSTIN COIL

"I PROMISED COIL A MILLION DOLLARS, AND HE PROMISED ME A CHAMPIONSHIP."

JOHN FORCE.NHRA.COM

John Force became a legitimate contender when he hired super tuner Austin Coil in 1985. Coil already had two Funny Car titles to his credit, and he maintained one of the busiest match-racing schedules on the circuit with the *Chi-Town Hustler*. *Jeff Burk*

By 1984, John Force was starting to make a name for himself in the drag racing world. With each race, he was getting better and better, and by the end of the year he had captured his first championship in the American Hot Rod Association (AHRA), a 10-race series some credit as the birthplace of modern drag racing.

Winning that championship only bolstered John's confidence more—enough that the charismatic racer decided to take his act to the NHRA. In 1984, he participated in 12 events, qualifying for 10 of them.

Yet Force's most trusted mentor, Gene Beaver, knew his young cousin needed a lot more guidance if his ability was ever going to catch up to his enthusiasm. As the 1984 AHRA season came to a close, Beaver introduced John to super-tuner Austin Coil.

"Guys were working in paint shops and car garages, and at night they were taking these pieces and creating something," Force said about the drag racing scene at the time in a Q&A for NHRA.com. "My team couldn't do that. That's why Gene Beaver told me to come over to where he was standing and take a look at something. He told me, 'Well, you can't hire Don Garlits because he's the best. But you could hire that guy, Austin Coil."

"I don't know if Beavs gets enough credit for all he did for John," promoter Steve Querico says in reflection. "He was a creative genius and the brains behind the early part of John's career. He was always steering John in the right direction."

So John wasted no time in approaching the mild-mannered Coil, who was sitting on the back of a truck eating his lunch. Force, never short on words, came right to the point.

"I said, 'I want to hire you.' He looked at me and said, 'Why would I possibly want to work for you?' And I told him, 'Cause I've got a million bucks,' which I lied about. But Beaver told me to look at what he is doing. He was eating a hot dog and at the same time, he had one piston and he was filing on it. Beaver said, 'That guy knows how to make a car run, just like Don Garlits. He doesn't have fifty pistons like some other guys. He's got one because he is broke and he has got to make it live.'"

THE GOSPEL ACCORDING TO JOHN

"YOU CAN TELL THE CHAMPIONS JUST BY LOOKING IN THEIR TRAILERS. THE FIFTH-PLACE GUY WILL HAVE FOUR FISHING POLES, THE SECOND-PLACE GUY MIGHT HAVE TWO, BUT IF YOU LOOK IN THE CHAMPION'S TRAILER, YOU WON'T FIND ANY."

— RACINGONE.COM

Running an Olds Firenza in the 1987 season with Castrol as the primary sponsor, John collected his first career NHRA national event victory at Montreal's le Grandnational against Ed "The Ace" McCulloch. *Jon Asher*

Coil, a former car dealership line mechanic who grew up in the Logan Square area of Chicago, had been working on Funny Cars since the mid-1960s. Racing with fellow Chicagoans John Farkonas and Pat Minick in the 1970s, Coil was the mastermind and one-third owner behind the famed *Chi-Town Hustler*, tuning driver Frank Hawley to a pair of NHRA Funny Car championships in 1982 and 1983.

"In the heyday of the *Chi-Town Hustler*, if you didn't run a national event, you could run three match-race dates the same weekend for fifteen hundred dollars apiece," Coil says. "So, we'd go run our booked-in deal and know we were coming home with forty-five hundred dollars.

Force and Coil maintained a grueling match-racing schedule—in part to make the money needed to run the team and in part to give John the lessons he needed to succeed on a variety of tracks in a variety of conditions. *Jon Asher*

Austin Coil, a former car dealership line mechanic from Chicago, began working on Funny Cars in the mid-1960s. An immediate mentor and coach to John, he gave John the cars and the mental toughness to be a winner. *Jeff Burk*

Back then, even at Indy, if you won, you didn't get any money, just a trophy."

The team, however, went winless at NHRA national events in 1984, and money earned from the busy match-racing schedule—nearly 100 events in their busiest year—was drying up as the NHRA grew in stature. When driver Frank Hawley decided to move on to open a drag racing school, Coil's future in racing was uncertain at best.

"We didn't have enough money to continue to run the NHRA series with the *Chi-Town Hustler*," Coil says. "So, I was somewhat more receptive to going in a different direction."

Austin Coil built John's racing program from scratch. He had no use for most of the parts and pieces Force had stockpiled before his arrival. *Ron Lewis*

The eyes of a champion. When no one else believed, John did.
Ron Lewis

Force promised to deliver the money if Coil came to work.

"Force called me every twenty minutes for two weeks," Coil told the *Los Angeles Times.* "When he finally made me an offer, I told him I needed about a week to think about it. He hung up and called me every twenty minutes until I said yes."

The deal, though, did not come without some conditions from Coil. He was going to make sure he was only responsible for one thing—bringing the hot rod to life on the racetrack.

"That was part of the agreement for me to come work here. It wasn't exactly a given," Coil said in that interview. "One of the first deals I made was [that] I don't travel in the truck. I don't wash, polish, lift, carry, push, tote, nothin'. That's what I do, and if you want to hire me for that, we can negotiate. If you don't, I'll just stay and run my own team. I really didn't know what I was getting into. He'd never won a national event, although he had been in a couple of final rounds."

"Coil said if I'm going to work for you, you have to agree to let me teach you how to drive," Force told the *Los Angeles Times.* "That's when he put a throttle stop on the car. That's when we ran Odessa, El Paso, every [bad track] across the country, and I said, 'Why are we running all these junk racetracks? They don't pay enough money.' He said because if you can learn to run on every track in the country, when you get to those national events when it rains, you'll be able to go right down a slick road."

John cut corners everywhere he could to pay Coil. He gave up his apartment and lived at the race shop or in the truck, subsisting on a diet of burgers, tacos, boiled eggs, and diet soda. John even drove his own transporter to save money, and it wasn't uncommon for the entire crew to share a single hotel room, taking mattresses off box springs to create the illusion of four beds. John would take a pillow and sleep in the tub.

Despite the financial limitations, drag racing's newest odd couple went to work—Coil training his driver and tuning the hot rod and Force looking for the additional funding it was going to take to build a winning program. They'd race anywhere there was guaranteed money, and Force was always on the lookout for sponsorship opportunities. Both men knew they were starting from scratch with this latest venture.

"One of the first deals I made [with Force] was that I don't travel in the truck. I don't wash, polish, lift, carry, tote, nothin'." — Austin Coil
Jeff Burk

"ANYBODY CAN DRIVE A GOOD RACE CAR (FROM) A TO B ON A GOOD RACETRACK. WHAT SEPARATES THE RACERS FROM THE DRIVERS IS WHAT THEY DO WHEN THE CAR GETS IN TROUBLE."

– TEAM CASTROL PRESS RELEASE

"They didn't have anything here that I wanted to use, and John expected that," Coil told *National Dragster.* "John's job, when I first got here, was to be busy all the time trying to sell everything he had. He never expected me to use anything he already had. We went shopping and got what I was used to running, and we put a car together. We started from scratch and worked our way up."

In 1986, John tried to get a meeting with Castrol Oil's John Howell to secure sponsorship dollars.

"He was a hard guy to get away from," Howell told the *Las Vegas Review Journal.* "Every time I'd walk past his trailer, I'd walk faster, but never fast enough. He'd always come out like he had radar. I think I gave him the deal [worth about $5,000] just to get rid of him."

Far from an instant success, John Force went 34 NHRA events without a victory before he teamed with Coil and ended up running another 31 with his new crew chief before capturing his

In 1987, John scored four runner-up finishes in addition to his win in Canada, giving him a fourth-place finish in the NHRA Funny Car points standings for the second consecutive year. *Jon Asher*

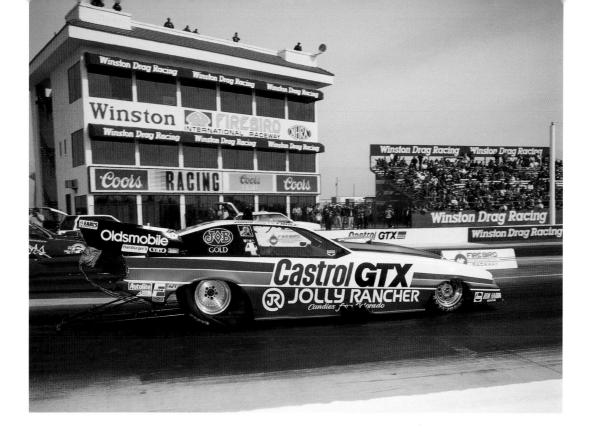

By the end of the 1987, Force and his wife Laurie had two daughters, Ashley and Brittany, with another, Courtney, on the way. With John on the road so often, Laurie thought the A-B-C names for the girls would help John remember them. *Jon Asher*

first final-round win light. In 1986, Force and Coil scored one No. 1 qualifier, making it to three final rounds but coming up empty each time.

"I promised Coil a million dollars, and he promised me a championship," Force recalled for NHRA.com. "But when we went through two seasons and hadn't won anything, I whined to him that he promised to make me a winner. He looked at me with that ol' toothpick sticking out of his mouth and said, 'Yeah, and you promised me a million dollars.'"

But on June 28, 1987, at Montreal's le Grandnational, John was sitting in his Olds Firenza waiting for a final-round matchup with Ed "The Ace" McCulloch at Sanair International Raceway. Kenny Bernstein and his famed Budweiser King Buick, Don Prudhomme and Billy Meyer already were on their trailers ready to go home. Force had been in this position nine times before, and each time he lost. Sometimes, he had the better car. Several times, he was expected to win. None of it had mattered. He had never gone all the way through an NHRA national event without tasting defeat.

There was nothing special about that day in Canada. In fact, it was dreary and raining most of the weekend. The conditions, along with a new concrete launching pad, were making the track unpredictable at best, playing right into the hands of Force and Coil, the only NHRA regulars still running a full match-race schedule.

"I sat back there [during the first session] and watched all three cars in front of me smoke the tires on the line," Force told *National Dragster.* "I looked over to Austin and said, this reminds me of Tucson [a now-closed Arizona track known for its lack of traction]."

John's matchups with nemesis Al Hofmann were often spectacular. "He's a helluva racer, he's marketed himself well, and he does the kind of interviews that attract attention and money," Al Hofmann says. *Ron Lewis*

"Austin said, 'Well then drive the car like it is Tucson,' and I went out and made a half-throttle launch and ran 5.78. When no one else made it down that lane, we felt we had a little edge on everyone and couldn't wait to run the right lane."

For the final round, the track was different still.

"Austin told me to just imagine that I was in my lane at Englishtown [New Jersey]," Force said, referring to his impressive match-race win streak at the New Jersey track. "He told me not to get worked up about winning my first national event, just to relax and do the job like I would anywhere else."

Force let Coil know that he took the advice to heart as he approached the car before the run. Laughing, Force said, "I want to win more than anything in the world, but I've been sick so many times and I'm so used to losing, I'm going to go up there and have some fun today because I'm in the final."

John talks with NHRA drag racing broadcaster Steve Evans. Force waited a long time to get into the television spotlight, and once he got a taste, his star power was undeniable. *Jon Asher*

A new sense of calm had come over the frenetic Force, and when Ed McCulloch went up in smoke off the starting line, John cruised to an easy win and his first national event trophy. Of course, Force was ready for his moment in the spotlight.

"[He] was running around looking for Steve Evans to interview him," Force's friend Bob Fisher told the *Las Vegas Review-Journal*. "But the race was in Canada, and it wasn't being televised."

"I was looking around for a TV commentator to do my interview, and there was nobody down there but a couple of drunk Canadians," Force added. "For years, I'd been practicing the winner's circle interview I was going to give Steve Evans, then the first race I win is the one that doesn't have TV." The rest of the world would have to wait a little longer to meet John Harold Force.

In 1988, Force and Coil chalked up three more wins together—the Spring Nationals, Northstar Nationals, and Winston Finals—and John finished third in the Winston Championship

Austin Coil is the calm to John Force's storm. The perfect combination of driver and crew chief is elusive at best, impossible to many. *Jeff Burk*

points race. His enthusiasm and ability were beginning to come together, a balance between high-energy pitchman out of the car and mind-over-matter nerves of steel behind the wheel.

"When you win, you get calmness," Force said in the *Brute Force* video. "When you get calm, you are at your best."

Part of that calmness came from the mental tricks Force and Austin used to eliminate the excitement and fear once he strapped into the car.

"I go against someone who has put a couple of lights on me and beat me up, and that guy comes up in the numbers again, and I got him, and that old heart starts beating and the fear comes back. You tell yourself, *Wait a minute, don't do what you know you can't do, and that's lose mental control.* You've got to come in here and dance and do your game," Force said in one interview. "I [visualize] my children and I get happy. I'm doing the burnout, backing up, I'm not

Despite earning a national event win in 1987, John Force was still years away from running for a championship. So Force kept up the hunt for more sponsor money, while Coil concentrated on building a winning operation. *Jon Asher*

As John gained experience and confidence, the pre-race burnouts got longer and smokier. It was the burnouts that impressed Force the most as a kid watching through the fence, and he made a point of delivering the same show for his fans. *Jon Asher*

Austin Coil may be better than anyone at matching the car to the track, and the car to the driver. Before each run, he tells John how the car is going to respond and he's rarely wrong. *Jeff Burk*

looking at the oil pressure, I ain't lookin' at nothin'. I'm thinking about my kids and wondering what they're doing, wondering if they're sitting at home watching TV, watching their crazy ol' man live. And pretty soon, I notice there is no sweat. There is calmness.

"In the old days, I'd pretend it was Freddie Krueger in the next lane because I didn't want to imagine that it was really Don Prudhomme. Because Don Prudhomme beat me up so many times, he was gonna beat me up again. Well, then don't make it Don Prudhomme. Put Shirley Temple over there. Mentally, put Shirley Temple in that car, and what are you afraid of?"

John believed he could be a champion when no one else did. Officials tried to keep him off the track, sponsors dodged him, and drivers laughed at his antics. But John stayed focused on getting the job done. *Jon Asher*

"John was John ten years before Austin Coil came along," former teammate Tony Pedregon once said. ". . . What broadened that was when he started winning and getting out and screamin' and hollerin'— all of a sudden, people thought this guy was good and entertaining." *Jon Asher*

Are those clouds in the sky, or just the results of another stellar burnout? *Ron Lewis*

Soon the team appeared to be off and running, and fans were starting to notice.

"John was being John ten years before Austin Coil came along," fellow NHRA driver Tony Pedregon says. "He had the same energy and probably had the sense of humor, but what broadened that was when he started winning and getting out and screamin' and hollerin'. All of a sudden, people thought this guy was good and entertaining."

Well, almost everyone thought it was entertaining. Some of his competitors took exception to the circus-like behavior. "He was a character from the very beginning," NHRA founder Wally Parks says. "But I believe he was quite disliked by the other drivers because he talked so much."

In 1989, however, Force was briefly humbled, making it to only two final rounds, collecting a late-season win at Reading and a runner-up at the Winston Finals. Force's championship and Coil's million dollars would remain on hold for at least another season.

John won seven times in seven final rounds the next year, defeating five different drivers: Bruce Larson at Houston, Texas, and Sonoma, California; Mark Oswald at Montreal, Canada, and Reading, Pennsylvania; Richard Hartman at Baton Rouge, Louisiana; Jim White at Columbus, Ohio; and Ed McCulloch at Brainerd, Minnesota. With four races remaining in the season, John held a slim points lead over The Ace, the man he had defeated for his first career win just a few years earlier.

At the 1990 season finale in Pomona, John Force had monumental day. He qualified in the No. 2 spot, but more importantly, clinched his first NHRA Funny Car championship. Finally, the

John and Austin spent years putting together the best of the best, and both did what they did best. Austin tuned the cars. John found the money to pay for everything. It's a formula that continues to work today. *Ron Lewis*

Austin's is the last voice John hears before each run, giving both men absolute trust in the other. *Jon Asher*

kid from Bell Gardens, who stared through cracks in the fence to see the long, smoky burnouts of his heroes, now ruled the world he only dreamed about as a kid.

Reflecting on the season, John pinpointed the moment he believed his team was ready to be the best in the business. A catastrophic engine explosion at Brainerd sent him to the hospital with minor burns and left his team with a smoldering pile of parts that the crew had to turn back into a race car by the next day.

"That's what won the first championship," Force said on NHRA.com. "It would have been easy to just park it [for the weekend]. If we had done that, Ed McCulloch probably would have won [the title] because we only beat him by a couple of rounds [44 points in today's system]. But we put it back together and went back out there and won the race. That's when I knew we had magic."

BUILDING A DYNASTY

"I JUST LOVE TO DRIVE AND I COULDN'T STAND THE IDEA OF SITTING HOME WHEN THERE WAS A RACE TO RUN."
— JOHN FORCE, *LOS ANGELES TIMES*

When John Force started winning races and collecting trophies, there was no stopping him. Once he tasted victory, he had no other goal in life than to be the absolute best in the business. *Ron Lewis*

John won seven times in 1990, defeating five different drivers in the finals. He collected five more trophies in 1991, earning back-to-back NHRA Funny Car championships. *Jon Asher*

John Force followed his first championship season with another title run in 1991, winning five races and making it to 10 final rounds in 18 events. By this time, nearly all the drivers on the circuit could see just how far Force would go to be a winner.

"We were racing John for the title, and we had just won a couple of events in a row," says Funny Car driver Mike Dunn, who piloted the Snickers Funny Car in 1991. "My owner at the time, E. B. Abel, had a Learjet, and he loved John Force. So, he talked John into going fishing. Mr. Abel's idea of fishing was to get in the Learjet, fly down to the Chesapeake Bay, charter a boat, and go out and fish for whatever the heck we were fishing for that day.

"So, we get on the jet, and Force, as paranoid as he is, starts wondering what we're really up to. The pilot gets on the jets with full brake and full throttle until it starts vibrating on the runway. He lets off the brake and does a Connie Kalitta liftoff at about forty-five degrees, sets us back in the seats, and John starts yelling at us that we're screwing with him to take his mind off the championship."

Eventually, the threesome found its way to the Chesapeake, and it didn't take long for the testosterone levels to rise, turning a casual day of fishing into another all-out contest for bragging rights.

"None of us were real big fisherman, but with John, naturally, it became a competition," Dunn says. "Well, we all caught fish. Everyone caught at least one, and most of us caught more

When John was a teenager, his car served as his bedroom, his homework desk, and his closet, among other things. So it's no surprise he now feels more at home in the cockpit of his Funny Car than he does any other place. *Jeff Burk*

Never camera shy, John makes any reporter's job easy, answering questions nobody asks, telling stories about times long forgotten, or just rambling on about things that pop into his head. *Jon Asher*

Shortly after Bernie Fedderly was let go by Larry Minor in the middle of the 1992 season, John added Cruz Pedregon's former crew chief to the Force camp. *Jon Asher*

than one. We're putting the fish in the freezer and John holds up a fish and said, 'I won. I caught the biggest fish.' The only problem was [that] it was my fish. But John had put his wristwatch around the tail of the biggest fish, and said, 'No, it's my fish. I put my watch on it to mark it.'"

"That's what John Force is all about," Dunn adds. "Even when we are talking about some old fish, he's going to do whatever it takes to win."

For Force and Austin Coil, though, racing was about much more than winning. It was about dominating. So, coming off back-to-back Funny Car titles, Force and company wanted to send a message in 1992.

"You can't start to think that anything is good enough other than total, complete domination," Coil says. "The only thing good about losing . . . you wind up going home with your tail between your legs saying, 'I can't allow this to ever happen to me again.' You need to be right on the edge all the time, and you need to treat every run like it is the final run at Indy. If you do, at least you know you've given your best."

In 1993, John bounced back after losing the championship to Cruz Pedregon with a dominant performance. Opening the season with six wins in the first seven events, the team went on to collect 11 national event wins in 13 trips to the final round. *Jeff Burk*

John scored his first career win at the prestigious U.S. Nationals in 1993 when his opponent, Kenji Okazaki, developed a fuel leak and couldn't make the final-round pass. *Jeff Burk*

During one stretch in 1993, John won five consecutive national events, beginning with the Slick 50 Nationals in early March and ending when he fell to Gordon Mineo in the first round of the Oldsmobile Springnationals in mid-June. *Jeff Burk*

The aggressive approach, however, got the team into early trouble in 1992.

"We tried to blow people away early in the season," Force said in a midseason story for *National Speed Sport News.* "It didn't work like we expected. People like [Al] Hofmann were using consistency, not making mistakes, to win."

Maybe trying a bit too hard, Force uttered his famous "I saw Elvis at a thousand feet" remark after his hot rod erupted in flames and crashed into the wall at 280 miles per hour at the Mid-South Nationals in Memphis. When his car finally came to rest, the sport's ultimate showman played to the home crowd, claiming to have seen a vision of The King during the fiery incident.

"It was kind of like running full speed across your living room and diving head first into the fireplace," Force told the *Los Angeles Times.* "I got out, and the local TV guy was standing right there in shock, holding the microphone, and the first thing I said was, 'Are we live?'"

The showmanship and the winning continued. After Force collected his third national event win of the season with a final-round victory over Hofmann at Canada's Sanair International Raceway, it looked like more of the same for the Castrol GTX Olds Cutlass and its crew, as they jumped out in front of the Funny Car points battle. But while Force was busy keeping one eye on Hofmann, a second-generation rookie behind the wheel of the Larry Minor–owned McDonald's Olds was quietly keeping pace.

Cruz Pedregon, son of Flamin' Frank Pedregon, was piloting the ride vacated by McCulloch's move to Top Fuel. Larry Meyer had taken over crew chief duties on the car midway through season, after Minor fired Bernie Fedderly. The new pairing had already started to make a little noise as they prepared to roll into Brainerd for the Champion Auto Stores Nationals. Fedderly, meanwhile, who had been with Minor for 10 years and two championships, didn't waste time finding employment, quickly teaming with Coil and the Force camp.

Before the Brainerd showdown, Cruz Pedregon and his team participated in a pit crew challenge at the Hilton Metrodome in the Twin Cities. During the event, Cruz Pedregon's hot rod was shut off to adjust the idle, and making a critical error, nobody on the crew backed the engine down to drain fuel from the cylinders. When the car was restarted, a massive explosion inside the 5,000-horsepower engine sent pieces of shrapnel into both Pedregon and Meyer, earning both a trip to nearby Hennepin County Medical Center. After digging metal fragments from Pedregon's hand, doctors cleared the Moorpark, California, driver to race that weekend. And race he did. With John Force being eliminated in the second round by Mark Oswald, Pedregon beat Oswald in the final round, cutting Force's points lead to 758.

"We were throwing wild cowboy punches out there and just missing by a little bit," Pedregon says. "We felt we had the ability, and we knew if we could get on a roll, we could do some damage. John's strength was consistency, but we felt like on a fast track, we had a car that could run with, and at times outrun, John's car. It gave us some confidence. As crazy as it sounds, we were thinking championship. But you have to think that way."

At Indy, one of the cowboy punches connected, as Pedregon turned in a dominant performance at the prestigious U.S. Nationals, becoming the first driver in NHRA history to record four consecutive runs with E.T.s below 5.20 seconds.

"John came out and won the Big Bud Shootout, and we thought we were going to get our rear end handed to us," Pedregon says. "But we got our act together on race day. We stumbled in the Bud Shootout, but we learned from it, and showed up on Labor Day and cleaned house."

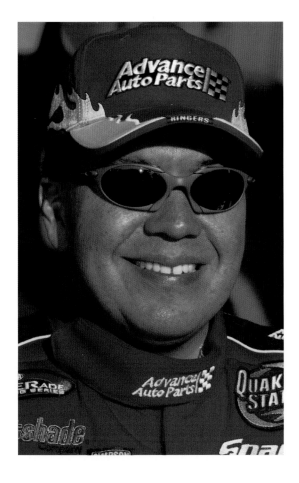

Cruz Pedregon and his McDonald's Olds provided the only bump in the road for Force, as John won every championship in the 1990s but one—the 1992 title, when Cruz took the title with a late-season flurry of victories. *Ron Lewis*

In the finals, Pedregon picked up an easy win over a tire-smoking Del Worsham and dug deeper into Force's lead, saying in a post-race interview, "I like our chances because we are going to tracks that favor our car."

The statement proved prophetic, as Pedregon earned his third consecutive victory, and fourth of the season, beating Hofmann at the Sunoco Keystone Nationals in Maple Grove, Pennsylvania. Again doing it in dominant fashion, Pedregon became the first Funny Car driver in NHRA history to run under 5.10 seconds—and he did it twice to set the record.

Force, who was running well all weekend, suffered mechanical problems in the second round and watched his points lead disappear to the McDonald's car he began referring to as "the hamburger from hell." As the Force banter picked up, Pedregon and his team took a different approach.

"Most of my team had been there through the McCulloch years," Pedregon says. "They knew Force and they were oblivious to his comments. I wanted to be humble. I wanted this to be a surprise attack. I wanted to come off as this shy kid—I was playing that up as much as John was playing up his end—I just stayed quiet. And I think the more quiet I was and the more I didn't respond to what he was saying, the more it affected him and not me.

"The last thing I wanted to do was get into any kind of exchange with him. I wanted him to think I was this quiet guy who didn't know much. I always gave John his credit and showed him the proper respect. There were times when I wanted to toot our horn a little more than I did, but ultimately I believed it would be to our advantage to stay quiet. Ultimately, it was."

As the NHRA packed up and headed for Heartland Park in Topeka, Kansas, the kid who had grown up watching Force from the stands was leading the defending champ by 438 points. Over the season's final three events, the battle became a full-scale war.

"I could tell that John had gone from happy-go-lucky to happy and pissed off," Pedregon says.

The truth of the matter was that Force was more than pissed off—he was obsessed with fear. "It was war," he said in an interview in *Performance Trends*. "I've got to fight. I fought twenty years to get here. Now, it's all slipping away to some kid driving a hamburger stand. [My kids] were saying, 'You'll be champ again, Daddy! And if you aren't, you'll have more time at home.' No, you don't understand. If they take away my championship, I lose my life."

"John works so hard and is on the road so much because he lives in fear that somebody's going to take it all away from him, and he's going to have to go back to driving a truck," his wife, Laurie, said in the interview with *USA Today*. "I ask him, when will you be able to enjoy everything you have worked for?"

Force, aware of the tradeoffs he's made in life, responded, "I probably won't enjoy it. I'll probably fall over dead one day, and my kids will enjoy it."

In the same *USA Today* story, Laurie shared a story about daughter Ashley describing her dad to first-grade classmates. "She told them her daddy was a big-old green and white race car, and that she didn't see him very often."

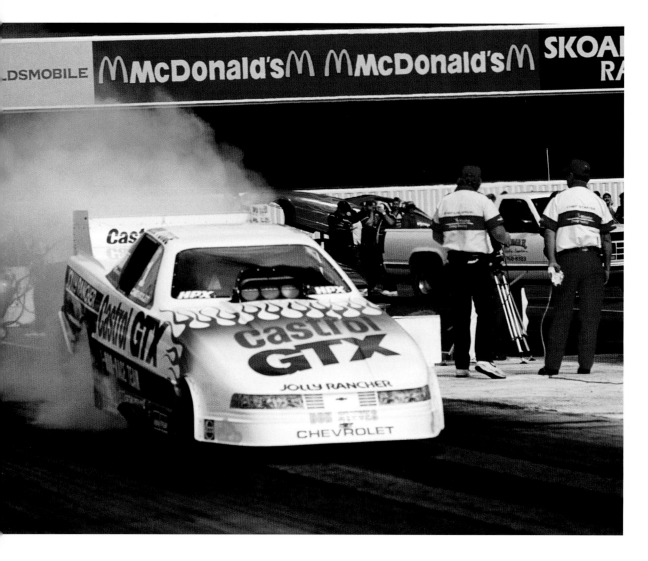

John set national records for speed (303.95 miles per hour) and elapsed time (4.93 seconds) as he hawked T-shirts touting "The Nightmare Continues" in 1994. *Jeff Burk*

Don Steves' tiny La Habra, California, Chevy dealership started with a showroom that had room for only one car. Steves was one of John's first sponsors and stayed with him even after Force switched to Ford.

Yes, life on the road was tough on the family, but John loved it. So when he went up against Pedregon in the final, he didn't think he would lose. But the Castrol Cutlass' engine blew up just before the finish line. His car in flames, John managed to climb out unscathed, thanks in large part to a new cowling his crew had installed to protect his head. The only part touched by the flames was the top of Force's helmet.

"I could see his fender, so I knew it was a close race." Pedregon recalls. "I remember crossing the finish line and being so elated, but as his car went by me, I could feel the heat, through my helmet shield, through my fire suit. He crossed over into my lane in a ball of fire, and I'm thinking, 'Oh my God—this guy is going to kill himself trying to beat us. They were laying it down. They did not want to give up that championship."

With two races to go in the 1992 season, Force trailed Pedregon by 686 points, and Pedregon was beginning to let his confidence show. "He has the crown, and we want to rip it off his head," he said in *National Speed Sport News* magazine.

At the Texas Motorplex, Force again met Pedregon in the finals, this time adding an incredible show for the fans in attendance.

"I remember walking up to the starting line with my wife, Sharon, and there was so much pressure," Pedregon recalled. "I've never had a race that had more riding on it in my life. We were like two gladiators. It was really that dramatic to me and to a lot of the people watching.

"I remember pulling up in the van and taking a deep breath. I got out and started to put my helmet on, and right as I am about to do that, John yells over, 'Hey Cruz, let's go to work.' He kept his composure. He kept his sense of humor, even in the most pressure-packed moments."

As both cars left the starting line, Pedregon's hot rod broke a fitting and sprayed water on the tires, causing him to smoke the tires early in the run. Ready to admit defeat, he looked up to see Force lose control of his car, slamming twice into the left-side guardrail. Pedregon got back in the gas. Force stayed with his car. Pedregon crossed the finish line first. Pedregon's fifth consecutive national event win had already been secured, however, as Force's contact with the wall had disqualified him. After the race, Force drove himself to a nearby hospital, where he was treated and released for a minor concussion.

"He was driving that car like a guy possessed," Pedregon says. "I think he was feeling our heat, but it actually did more for his fan base. It was like a boxer getting knocked out of the ring and coming back in to keep fighting. I watch the video of that race today and it makes the hair on my arm stand up."

With one race remaining on the schedule, Force needed a miracle at the Winston Finals. The Pomona weekend got off to a rough start for the defending champion, as John lost control of his car during qualifying at the Los Angeles County Fairplex, flipped it on its roof, spun around, and crossed the finish line upside down.

"He jumps out of the car, throws his arms in the air. You'd think the Dallas Cowboys just scored the winning touchdown," says Pedregon, who was lined up directly behind Force in the next pairing. "I was wearing earplugs, and I could hear the roar of the crowd. I'm thinking to myself, 'What else can happen? I'm not a fearful person, but this guy was crazy."

When Force broke a blower belt in the first round of eliminations against Gary Bolger, the battle was over, and all hopes of a third title were gone. Pedregon, a former diesel truck racer, had come from more than 1,600 points behind with seven races remaining to take the crown.

"I'm glad this one is over," John said after the race. "This is one of those seasons you just survive. We've got a lot of work to do for next year."

In 1993, Force put his determination to return to the top on display early, winning the season-opening Winternationals over Worsham on a hole shot. He and Coil opened the season with six wins in the NHRA's first seven events and finished the season with 11 national event wins in 13 trips to the finals. Despite the early season success, however, the loss of the 1992 title to Pedregon still weighed heavy on John's mind.

Traveling from Sonoma with Laurie and their three daughters to Seattle, John pulled into a McDonald's in Oregon.

"McDonald's was having a promotion where their Happy Meals contained Cruz Pedregon Funny Cars," public relations specialist Paul Kelly says. "The girls were playing with the cars in the back seat, when John noticed what they were playing with. John pulled over on the side of

" . . . I REALLY BELIEVE YOU CAN BE A DRAG RACER AND BE HOME TO BARBECUE. BUT IF YOU WANT TO BE A CHAMPION, YOU HAVE TO GIVE UP YOUR LIFE."

— LOS ANGELES TIMES

the road, pulled the car out of his daughters' hands, dropped it on the ground, and started stomping on it. He totally crushed it, yelling the entire time about how Cruz was ruining his life. He left the plastic wreckage on the side of the road and continued on with the trip. Somewhere along the line, Laurie convinced him that he had overreacted. Feeling a bit ashamed, but no less the warrior, John pulled into another McDonald's and replaced the cars."

"I think John will always be a little bit afraid of Cruz," Kelly adds. "It doesn't matter if Cruz has less money or a weaker team, I think John knows Cruz is the one driver who can drive a Funny Car as well as he can. John Force will always worry about Cruz Pedregon for the length of their careers."

Later that summer, Force was able to put some of those demons to rest. At Indy, he won drag racing's Super Bowl, the U.S. Nationals, when final-round opponent Kenji Okazaki developed a fuel leak and couldn't make the pass in the opposite lane. It was Force's first win at the event, after 13 appearances in a Funny Car. Again the class of the field, John Force left Indianapolis with a nearly insurmountable points lead over Pedregon and the rest of the chasers, but the season would not go without some major disappointments.

Calling his October trip to Heartland Park "the worst weekend of his life," John could only watch as Chuck Etchells became the inaugural member of the Castrol 4-Second Club, earning a $25,000 bonus with a run of 4.907 seconds. Ironically, Force had put up half of the prize money himself, with his sponsor Castrol putting in the rest. Both had the full expectation that the money would come back to the team. Writing the check to Etchells was especially painful, as he was sponsored by rival oil company, Kendall. So Force and his team turned their attention to the 300 miles-per-hour barrier, a mark not yet reached by a Funny Car driver. Jim Epler, however, beat him to the punch, running a 300.40 during Sunday's first round of eliminations.

"I might as well kill myself," John said in an interview after the event. "I had everything. Now, it's all gone. Those other guys, Etchells and Epler, they did great. But it makes me sick." Force did earn a highlight two weeks later, though, as he became the second member of the Castrol 4-Second Club and the first to set an E.T. below five seconds (4.996).

John was named the Funny Car Driver of the Year on the annual *Car Craft* magazine All-Star Team. *Jon Asher*

In the fall of 1995, Force began to consider expanding to a two-car operation, a move that earned him unfair criticism from competitors, but he certainly was not the first car owner to do it. *Jon Asher*

In 1994, Force's popular souvenir trailers were hawking T-shirts that read, "The Nightmare Continues." For his opponents, the phrase could not have been more true and, for some, beating John Force was becoming an obsession.

"I've seen Al Hofmann almost go crazy trying to beat him," says John McNichols, John's high school football coach and longtime friend. "I was afraid he was going to kill himself trying to beat John. He was so focused on beating John that he forgot other things. I'd grit my teeth when he was against John because I was afraid he was going to do things that made no sense."

John survived an early season "cheating" scandal in 1995, as other teams accused his Force team of using traction control. Force said that even his own children asked him if he was cheating.
Jon Asher

Austin Coil runs the show at John Force Racing, but co-crew chief Bernie Fedderly (pictured here) is an important part of the program. John Medlen was added at the end of the 1995 to run the team's second car.
Jon Asher

"I've always had a lot of respect for John," Al Hofmann admits. "He is a hard racer. You can't fault him for everything he's gone after. He's gone after the championships aggressively, where some people have been a little slack in that department. He's a helluva racer, he's marketed himself well, he does the kind of interviews that attract attention and money, and that's what it takes to run in the sport." With a chuckle, Hofmann added, "Next to me, he's the best driver out there. I think the world of the guy. I'd do anything for him or anything to him."

On the track, John was piloting a new Chevrolet Lumina, but the results were the same. The team continued to rip through the competition, winning 10 of the year's 19 events and setting national speed (303.95 miles per hour) and E.T. (4.93 seconds) records. All of this came in the shadow of his idol, Don Prudhomme, who was wrapping up his hall of fame career with his Final Strike tour.

At the Fram Southern Nationals in April, Force defeated Dean Skuza for his 35th career Funny Car victory, tying him with Prudhomme for first on the all-time list. In July, Force became the first racer to win at every NHRA track when he collected a win at Denver's Bandimere Speedway. He went on to sweep the NHRA Western Swing with wins at Sonoma and Seattle, and in August, he shared the stage with Prudhomme, as both were winners in Brainerd.

After the race, John shared his secret to summer success with the *Winston Drag Racing Review*. "Match racing—the car doesn't know it is this hot out. My guys know what to do to it

From left to right, the NHRA's winningest combination: Austin Coil, John Force, and Bernie Fedderly. *Ron Lewis*

when it gets this hot because we've been there," he said. "My guys know what to do. They say I work my crew too hard, but that's why we run like this."

The match-racing experience not only helped Force stay hot behind the wheel, but it also taught him a lesson or two about showmanship. Bill Bader, former IHRA president and Norwalk Raceway Park head honcho, recalls the first time he booked Force for a match race at the track's legendary Fourth of July celebration, Night Under Fire.

"When he showed up at the driver's meeting, I asked him if he was superstitious," Bader says. "He just laughed and said, 'Hey, listen. I crash 'em, I roll 'em, I flip 'em, I burn 'em—I'm not superstitious.'" Good thing, because Bader's script was a wild one.

"I told him we were going to bring him out in a coffin," Bader adds. "He said, 'I ain't getting in no damn coffin.'"

John ended the 1995 season with an unprecedented fifth NHRA Winston Funny Car title, moving him ahead of drag racing greats Don "The Snake" Prudhomme and Kenny Bernstein. *Jon Asher*

Bader's plan was to have fellow Funny Car driver Dean Skuza—dressed as an undertaker, complete with black tie and tails—drive in sitting atop a converted horse-drawn hearse wagon, now powered by a big Chevy engine. Force would be in the coffin in the back.

"They would be the last two guys we introduced to the crowd, and Dean would say over the P.A. system, 'Force, I'm here to bury you.' Force was then supposed to rise up out of the coffin in front of the crowd and reply, 'Skuza, I'm your worst nightmare,'" Bader says.

When the time came to get the stunt started, Force was still signing autographs. "I had to chase the people away and get John into the coffin," Bader says. "He barely fit. I handed him his microphone, rushed the top closed, and told Skuza to hit it. As he took off, everyone heard a loud grunt over the P.A. system, and I couldn't help but laugh because I was the only one that knew it was John hitting his head inside the coffin. But everything went off just as planned, and the fans loved it."

Force went on to clinch his fourth NHRA Winston Funny Car Championship at the 1994 Sears Craftsman Nationals with a simple first-round defeat of Ronny Young. He closed out the year a month later with an eye-popping night run of 303.95 miles per hour, the fastest run ever in a Funny Car. He finished the year with 42 career wins, earning half of those victories in his record-setting 1993 and 1994 seasons.

In 1995, Force and his gang were ready to continue kicking butt in the flopper division, running on top in preseason test sessions. Once the season got underway, though, Force found himself in the heat of controversy. A dropped cylinder at Pomona led to an uncharacteristic first-round loss for the defending champ, his first such early exit in more than eight months.

Following the season opener, NHRA tech director John Erickson blasted fuel teams with a warning that all cars would be subject to comprehensive searches for the remainder of the season. The target of the intense searches: traction-control devices that theoretically stop throwout-bearing movement, cutting power to the rear wheels without a driver having to lift off the accelerator.

"He denies it, but no matter what he says, I saw it on the car in Pomona," Al Hofmann says about Force. "They knew it was going to be checked, so it came off the car in Phoenix. It was off the car, but they definitely were fooling around with it. Hey, it ain't cheatin' until you get caught."

At the season's second event, the Atsco Nationals in Phoenix, John's fellow competitors felt like Team Force had been busted, as Force smoked the tires on three consecutive qualifying runs. In typical Force fashion, however, he came out swinging.

"My own children asked me if I was cheating," John said *National Speed Sport News*. "I even asked Austin and Bernie if we were cheating. They [The NHRA] even told me to undress one time [for a search]," Force continued. "So, I dropped my pants. All they saw was my Power Rangers underwear."

The critics, including Hofmann, were stunned and silenced when the self-proclaimed "driving Force of the 1990s" moved through the field and into the finals at Phoenix, piloting his clean machine to an event win over Tom Hoover with a run of 5.057 seconds at 298.30 miles per hour. A few weeks later, at the Gatornationals, the drama continued as Force destroyed a clutch in a semifinal win over Whit Bazemore. The team completed work on the damaged part with Force strapped in the car. A police motorcycle escort, sirens blaring, led the car to the starting line, where Force proceeded to collect his fourth consecutive Gainesville win.

"I EMBELLISH EVERYTHING, BUT ONE THING THAT'S FACT IS MY WIN-LOSS RECORD."

– JOHN FORCE, *USA TODAY*

Force once told the *St. Petersburg (Florida) Times*: "I want the Richard Petty image. I want the Elvis Presley following. When they bury me, buddy, I want the fans to come by and see me." *Ron Lewis*

The victory was the second of six on the season for John, including triumphs in Richmond, Virginia; Atlanta; Denver; and Brainerd. Force finished the season with 48 career national event wins and an unprecedented fifth NHRA Funny Car championship, moving ahead of drag racing giants Prudhomme and Kenny Bernstein.

In the fall of 1995, John Force began to consider building his dominant Funny Car team into a two-car operation. As the new reigning king of drag racing, he and his tactic received a lot of attention. Guys like Jack Roush and Larry Minor had run multi-car teams, but John Force would be the first to do so during the NHRA's era of television growth. He wanted a research and development machine with a young driver behind the wheel, and among the names considered for the ride was a then-30-year-old Top Fuel pilot named Ron Capps. Someone else, however, was hot for opportunity to team up with the champion, and a series of chance events solidified that connection for Force.

Tony Pedregon, Cruz Pedregon's kid brother, was driving a second car for Larry Minor at the time, and had just blown up his race car at Indianapolis. Tony was only in his first year behind the wheel of a Funny Car and now found himself in need of a new hot rod.

"I knew John had a brand new chassis. . . . He had developed a Camaro body that he couldn't use because he was with Pontiac at the time and couldn't get the funding from Chevrolet," Tony recalls. "I had heard through the grapevine that the car was just sitting there." So he made a deal with Minor to split the cost of buying the Force car.

"It was a [Steve] Pleuger chassis, but John's people set it up, and that's what we finished the year in," Pedregon adds.

Not one of the more social drivers on the circuit, Tony heard about Force's desire for a second team while reading in *National Speed Sport News* that Capps was getting the ride.

"I decided to get John's office number from Cruz and give him a call just in case," Tony says. "If he hadn't made his decision yet, I was just hoping my name might at least come up. I wanted to leave him a message to let him know I was interested."

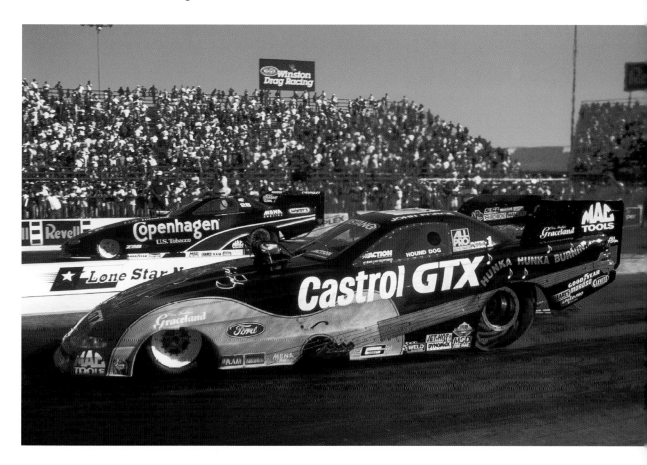

John has a passion for all things Elvis Presley—another truck driver with humble beginnings who eventually set the standard in his profession and developed an incredible fan following. *Ron Lewis*

John's big fear in life is that other drivers will figure out everything he knows. He is constantly looking to improve, bring in more brain power, and develop more horsepower. *Ron Lewis*

John won six times in 11 final rounds in 1995, but even after three strong seasons in a row, the best remained yet to come. *Jeff Burk*

At the same time, Minor was considering closing down Tony's Funny Car team in 1996, in order to spend more time with his family. When Force heard the veteran owner might have a trailer becoming available—Pedregon's trailer—he drove down to take a look. During the conversations, the topic of Force's new driver came up.

"Larry put a good word in for me and mentioned some of the qualities and abilities I had, just to work on the car," Pedregon says. "I think that's what Force was really looking for—someone who wouldn't tell him he wouldn't do this or that."

On Thanksgiving Day 1995, Force called Pedregon.

"I was with Cruz and all our families, and I checked my phone messages," Tony says. "At first, I thought it was a prank phone call. I recognized the voice, and he said, 'Hi Tony, this is

John handpicked second-generation driver Tony Pedregon to pilot his second car. In part because of Tony's talent, and in part to annoy his nemesis Cruz Pedregon—Tony's brother. *Jon Asher*

John Force. I'm adding a second team, and I'd like to interview you and consider you as a driver for that car. I'll call you back.'

"I hung up the phone and my family was just getting ready to sit down and eat. I told Cruz that I had a message from John, and he wanted to talk to me about driving the second car. I couldn't tell if Cruz was excited or he just lost his appetite."

Cruz Pedregon made sure his kid brother kept his name in the mix. "He told me to be relentless, just like Force was," Tony says. "He told me to call him and keep calling him. So I did. I called him every day. I tried not to be too annoying. So, when his daughter, Adria, would answer the phone, my message would be short, and I'd ask her to tell him I called."

Finally, Pedregon's persistence paid off. "Adria told John I was on the phone, and I could hear him in the background," Tony says. "He said, 'Tell him if I am hiring based on who calls me the most, he's got the job.'"

Force and Pedregon finally sat down together at the Yorba Linda race shop and talked informally about the job, with Force not totally committing to the partnership.

"Literally, I believed it was a month-to-month deal," Pedregon says. "In my conversations with John, he mentioned that maybe we'd run half of the schedule because, initially, he was funding the program out of his own pocket. But for me, at that stage of my career, I told John I was willing to do anything. I had a lot of experience working on cars, I had a little experience driving a Funny Car, and I had some Bud Shootout points to go with it."

"Tony's a very good driver, a pretty darn good race car mechanic, and he works well with the media, which is very important to John," Bernie Fedderly said regarding the partnership in the *Los Angeles Times*. "But did he also [hire Tony] to gnaw on Cruz a little? Probably."

Tony Pedregon started working with the team a few weeks later, tuner John Medlen was brought into the Force camp to work on the second car, and the relationship was set when teams began testing in Phoenix in the winter. It was the first time Pedregon had a chance to drive his new car, but on Friday, the first day of testing, Force took most of the runs in Pedregon's car.

"John was a little nervous the first time I got in the car," Pedregon recalls. "He started to tell me a few times that he had been having nightmares about me in the new car, but he held back. He just didn't want those thoughts in my head. The very first time I suited up, I got the helmet on, they towed me up to the starting line, right up to the pad, and John leaned in and said, 'Have fun.' I was nervous, but I was always nervous anyway. But I remember John saying, 'Have fun. Do your thing. You've driven these cars before.' Then he finished it off by saying, 'I'm buying.'

The plan was to run the car to 700 or 800 feet, with instructions from new crew chief John Medlen to run a little farther if things felt right. Pedregon was instructed to make a simple check-out pass and shut it off, but his first run ended up going all the way down the track. "It felt pretty damn good to me," Pedregon says. "The car ran a 4.99, which, at the time, was very impressive."

Force, in what became a tradition, rode his scooter to the end of the track to meet Pedregon. "His hair was flying all over the place," Pedregon says with a laugh. "He was obviously excited, and when he got down there, we were hugging and jumping all over the place. That was the start of everything."

THE QUEST TO BE THE BEST

"I LOVE WHAT I DO. YOU HAVE TO GO TO WORK, BUT THE BEST THING IS WORKING WITH THE PEOPLE AND THE FANS."
—JOHN FORCE, USA TODAY

John scored a career-defining season in 1996, on and off the track. He earned North American Driver of the Year honors and was the first drag racer ever to be so recognized by the distinguished panel of motorsports media members. *Jon Asher*

Every great athlete has an accomplishment, a streak, a moment in time that defines his or her professional career. For John Force, the 1996 season was that moment—when he demonstrated his total domination of a sport in which he had fought so hard just to participate in a decade earlier. He ruled on the track, he ruled with the fans, and he ruled the business of drag racing like no other driver in the history of the quarter-mile. The 1996 season was owned by John Force.

The season opened quietly enough in February, with longtime nemesis Al Hofmann knocking the defending champ out in the final round of the Winternationals. John had to wait until week two of the 1996 season to score his first victory, beating Chuck Etchells in the final round at Phoenix.

The media, used to an endless flow of quotable rants, colorful stories, and rapid-fire embellishments from Force, observed an absent and relatively quiet driver. It wasn't an accident. The Winston public relations team had taken away the champ's platform.

"John had hired Sid Morris to handle some of his business affairs," says public relations specialist Paul Kelly. "Sid felt as though John was getting big enough to be compensated more than any of the other drivers when he participated in NHRA media events. He even wanted John to be paid for his time on teleconferences. He wanted John to be paid for everything. We paid the drivers to come in for media day, but we didn't pay them to do phone interviews. [Former NHRA media relations manager] Denny Darnell was going to have none of that, so for the first two races, we didn't book John for any media appearances or phone calls. We didn't put John in front of a single reporter or fan. When John was not included on any teleconferences or any

In 1996, John was the first drag racer to win 13 races in a season, the first to reach 16 final rounds, and the first in a long time to clinch the championship by the Indy race. *Jon Asher*

John led the NHRA Funny Car points standings the entire year in 1997, setting speed records at three consecutive events. *Jon Asher*

John and his team scored the most lucrative drag racing weekend ever at Indy in 1996, earning $440,000 in prize money for winning both the U.S. Nationals and the Big Bud Shootout. NHRA bonuses, sponsor incentives, and contingencies also were part of the final tally. *Jon Asher*

Austin Coil handpicks his crew carefully, including Bernie Fedderly (pictured here). "We look for people with similar approaches in the way they handle their jobs," Coil once said. *Jon Asher*

John puts a lot of emphasis on a winning team, reading books about great winners, calling countless team meetings, and rewarding everyone from the crew chief to the receptionist when the team wins. *Jon Asher*

Tony Pedregon was relentless in his pursuit of the number two seat at John Force Racing, eventually winning the position and keeping it for eight seasons. *Ron Lewis*

event press conferences for the first two races, John called in a panic, wondering why he wasn't being given his traditional spot in front of the NHRA's marketing machine. Denny explained that if his management insisted on him being paid more than the other drivers, the NHRA would use the other drivers. I don't know what was said or done, but by Gainesville, John was back in the PR fold and it was business as usual. For John, attention and contact with the public is like oxygen. He lives for that interaction."

So by the time the Gatornationals got rolling, John, once again, was holding court with the media, and it was obvious he was taking everyone along for a nitro-powered ride.

As rain left teams uncertain of track conditions in Florida, John turned to his crew chief brain trust of Austin Coil, Bernie Fedderly, and newly added John Medlen.

"After the rain, I got a little nervous," John told *National Speed Sport News.* "How do you make a call on a track you're not sure of? I wanted to help. I told Austin I was the quarterback. He told me he was the coach—he made the call. Coil told me to relax an I knew it was going to set me back in my seat. He was right. It launched so hard my hands came off the wheel. It's a good thing I carried the front end about two-hundred feet while I was trying to get a hold of the wheel."

Force got both hands back in position and tightened his grip on the points lead, again beating Etchells, collecting his fifth consecutive Gatornationals victory with a run of 4.999 seconds at 301.40 miles per hour to Etchells' 5.232 at 302.01. The roll continued in Texas, as Force defeated

"Attention and contact with the public are like oxygen [for John]," says PR man Paul Kelly. **"He lives for the interaction. If he doesn't have it, he feels like he is going to die."** *Jeff Burk*

Hofmann to win the Slick 50 Nationals. But John made an even louder statement in Baytown that weekend, long before making it to the final round.

In his first elimination matchup with new teammate Tony Pedregon, Force quieted the talk that Tony would automatically lay down for the boss, as Tony ran a 5.159 at 300.30 miles per hour, nearly beating the man who had hired him.

"I hate it," John said at the time. "But when it comes down to it, you have to give young people who put their heart into it a chance. When we were sitting in the trailer, I said, 'Do your thing. Don't you dare red light on me, don't hit your parachute, and if I smoke the tires and you shut off, you'll ruin my career.'"

John dominated the Funny Car division in 1997 with six wins, ten final rounds, six No. 1 qualifying spots, seven low elapsed times, and five top speeds. *Jeff Burk*

John and new teammate Tony Pedregon finished 1-2 in the Funny Car points standings in both 1996 and 1997. *Jon Asher*

Force knew critics and competitors would raise a collective eyebrow at his use of a "blocker" to maintain his advantage, potentially questioning his position among the greats in the sport if he didn't earn every win. But it wasn't his enemies he was worried about. Force did not want to lose any of his fans.

"It isn't about winning," Force told *USA Today*. "When I am in the winner's circle, they're there, and when I am not, they are still at my trailer. It's about fan following."

So, despite Coil's protests, John insisted Tony race him all out at all times early in the season. Shortly after winning the Winston Select Invitational in Rockingham, North Carolina, however, Force started to rethink his position. In Atlanta, Tony and Force squared off in the final, with Tony taking the win. Force realized out loud, "I'm crazy. I've hired my own assassin."

Being pushed from inside his team as well as outside kept Force hungry and focused on the task at hand — pursuing the championship. It was a game of words and attitude, along with driving skills. After picking up victories in Richmond and Englishtown later in the spring, Force led Al Hofmann in the Winston Championship point standings by a comfortable 328 points. Hofmann thought a shot at the leader might help his cause.

"Fans are about Force'd out," Hofmann told the *New York Daily News*. Force, however, was up for a battle, too, offering vintage lessons in quarter-mile trash talking.

"You want to know the truth?" he asked an *Asbury Park Press* reporter. "It's about how many people are at the rope. When they leave, the sponsors that give you all the money, they're gonna leave, too. So, you're only worth the crowd. There will be two fans at [Hofmann's] ropes this weekend, and they'll both be his relatives. One will be trying to convince the other to come down to my trailer and see a nice guy. Al's nuts, but we love him."

John had always known early in his career the importance of relating to the fans. "You have to realize a woman will stand there for an hour with her hand through the ropes [to get an autograph] and then she will yell, 'I got it!' and she'll run off into the crowd," he said. "They can't get that close to Garth Brooks, but they can get that close to me. I ain't as cute, but they can get close."

At the next event, the rain-delayed Pontiac Excitement Nationals, Force lost in a tire-smoking quarterfinal to Chuck Etchells. However, both Hofmann and Cruz Pedregon struggled, and Force actually increased his lead, leaving Ohio with a 381-point advantage.

After beating his teammate in Memphis, Force turned in the performance of the season in Topeka, setting the E.T. record at 4.889 seconds, the first time a Funny Car had ever run below 4.90. In the final, Force defeated Pedregon in a blistering-fast matchup, running 4.930 at 303.54 miles per hour to Cruz Pedregon's 4.942 at 304.36 miles per hour.

John extended his lead to 500 points with a win at Bandimere to start the NHRA Western Swing, yet continued cautiously to avoid talk of a sixth championship. After Cruz Pedregon scored a victory in Sonoma, Force reminded his team of 1992 and the late-season comeback that Pedregon pulled off to win the Funny Car title.

In Brainerd, Force collected his 10th win of the season, mathematically eliminating all but the Pedregon brothers from competition. At this point, any talk of "ifs" and "maybes" was ridiculous at best. Cruz or Tony Pedregon would have to win every remaining race, setting national records

Despite starting the 1997 year in a Pontiac, Force and Pedregon finished the year in Fords. Force wanted Pontiac to step up support of the team's second car; when the manufacturer didn't, the team switched to Fords. *Jeff Burk*

By the mid-1990s, NHRA nitromethane-powered Funny Cars were hitting speeds in excess of 300 miles per hour, launching with G-forces equivalent to a space shuttle liftoff. *Ron Lewis*

Just another day at the office for the ol' truck driver. *Ron Lewis*

John Force has always made himself available to his fans. "They can't get that close to Garth Brooks, but they can get that close to me," he says. "I ain't as cute, but they can get close." *Ron Lewis*

THE GOSPEL ACCORDING TO JOHN

"PEOPLE DRIVE FOR HOURS TO SEE JOHN FORCE, TO GET MY AUTOGRAPH, AND THEY'RE GOING TO BE PISSED OFF IF I DON'T COME THROUGH. I DON'T WANT TO LET DOWN THE MAN WHO DROVE SIX HOURS WITH HIS KIDS AND SPENT HUNDREDS OF DOLLARS. THE DAY WILL COME THAT I'M NOT WORTH SHIT, BUT THEY'LL STILL LOVE ME." — *ST. PETERSBURG TIMES*

The only thing John Force does better than drive a race car is entertain a crowd. *Jon Asher*

Force struggled early in 1998, not winning until the eighth stop on the tour. *Jeff Burk*

Ron Capps, driving for Don "The Snake" Prudhomme, was one of several talented young drivers to challenge Force in the mid-1990s.
Jeff Burk

along the way, all the time hoping John Force would not win another elimination round.

At Indianapolis, Force put an end to any lingering doubt, putting on quite a show en route to sealing the deal for his sixth Winston Championship points title and scoring the most lucrative weekend in drag racing history along the way.

Over the Labor Day weekend, the team collected purse money for winning both the U.S. Nationals and the Big Bud Shootout, $50,000 from the NHRA for "doubling up," a $4,000 low-qualifier bonus, as well as contract incentives and product contingencies. The final haul was in the neighborhood of a half million dollars. The Indianapolis win was Force's record-tying 11th of the season in his record-tying 14th final of the year.

Off the track in 1996, business for Team Force appeared every bit as successful as the work at the races. After agreeing to in-season deals with Pontiac and Castrol, apparently extending those relationships into the new millennium, and signing a mega-deal with Action Collectibles and Hasbro on the merchandising side, Force, the "ol' truck driver" on the circuit, was running the show in American drag racing.

"Waterbed" Fred Miller, a crewman on the famous Blue Max Funny Car entry and the director of licensing for Action, at the time said this about Force: "This is the guy. As big as he is right now, he has the capacity to carry the program."

"John is a very good salesman," Tony Pedregon says. "When he finally gets the opportunity to go in and pitch a company on a winning proposition, he has the best of both worlds. He doesn't

At Indy, John and the team got back on track with a win over Randy Anderson to reclaim the points lead. *Jon Asher*

just sell it to the boardroom, but he has them walking out in stitches at the same time. I don't know anyone else that is able to do that. He's got something that no one else in this sport has to offer."

John Force ended the season as the first drag racer to win 13 races in a season, more than twice as many as the rest of his competitors combined. He was the first to be in 16 finals and the first in years to have a championship clinched by Indianapolis.

The epic season earned him driver of the year honors as the top racer in North America, an award whose past winners include Andretti, Petty, Earnhardt, Unser, Foyt, and Gordon. It marked the first time a drag racer had won the honor.

"It was my first year as a voting member of the driver of the year panel," says John Sturbin, motorsports reporter for the *Ft. Worth Star-Telegram*. "I was a little surprised to learn that no other drag racer had ever won the award. Not Don Garlits, not Shirley Muldowney, not [Bob] Glidden, not Snake [Prudhomme]. So for Force to be the first was really special. And in 1996, there was not a more deserving candidate. He totally dominated the sport. He had my vote."

As for that startup second car Force introduced early in the year—the one originally teased as a Veteran's Tour car before becoming the team's R&D machine—Tony Pedregon piloted the Force-owned Pontiac Firebird to a second-place points finish, behind his boss. Team Force didn't just beat the field in 1996; they buried it.

"You don't win six championships and the number of events he's won without being a great driver," Kenny Bernstein, a former Funny Car champion who beat Force with regularity early in John's career, told *USA Today*. "He's in that elite group."

In 1998, John won fewer races than both Ron Capps and Cruz Pedregon, but Force still won the championship. *Ron Lewis*

John's teams win races for a reason—they are dedicated. Often, the Force team arrives at the track first in the morning and they leave later than most teams at night. *Jeff Burk*

Symbols of greatness. *Ron Lewis*

Force's idol, Don Prudhomme, agreed. "When he started, he didn't have anything and didn't win for several years. He worked his way up, came up the hard way. He's earned every damn thing he's got."

As important, he knows how to hang on to what he has, including his sponsorships and key crew members.

"Every team has a sponsor and the sponsor pays the bills, but most teams are working on a one-year deal." Coil told RacingOne.com. "A few have two years, and there may be some out there I don't know about that are three years, but we have a five-year deal with our sponsor."

Coil says Force also takes the long-term contract approach with his team members. "So, even if a team came in and offered me twice as much money, I might make twice as much for one or two years, and then the deal is done, John hates me, and no one else can afford to pay me what I've been making, so I could really hurt my career for one year and a few bucks," Coil says. "Besides, with the machine Force has built here, why would you want to go anywhere else?"

"I would attribute the longevity of the Force team to John's care," adds longtime IHRA boss Bill Bader. "He recognizes them all as individuals. He listens to them. He is a voracious communicator, more than anyone I know. And when he's confronted with a tough situation, he goes right at it, where someone else might tend to ignore it, in hopes that it will work itself out. . . . Force never forgot where he came from."

"He knows how important it is to motivate his guys from top to bottom," public relations specialist Paul Kelly says. "He'll drive around all morning in his Viper, mainlining coffee and listening to James Brown belt out 'Living in America,' so that by the time he gets to the shop, he's fired up

John backed up all his talk, jumping out to an early points lead in 1999 with the new Roush-designed Mustang. *Carol Johnson*

"I ALWAYS WORE A SEIKO BECAUSE I THOUGHT THAT WAS THE BEST THERE WAS. HELL, I DON'T NEED NO WATCH THAT WORKS ON THE MOON. I AIN'T GOIN' THERE."
— JOHN FORCE, *LOS ANGELES TIMES*

Many years and many dollars removed from his humble trailer-park beginnings, John still feels at home on the road and on the move. *Jeff Burk*

John chats with his idol, Don "The Snake" Prudhomme. There were discussions about Prudhomme coming out of retirement for a one-time-only match race with Force at Indy, but the event never came to fruition. *Jeff Burk*

and transferring that caffeine-powered enthusiasm to every person he comes in contact with. He knows it all starts and ends with him."

In return, though, Force demands total dedication from his crew. Rumor holds he once fired an employee for bringing a fishing pole to work, saying, "We're not here to catch bass, we're here to win championships."

"It takes years to build a crew and camaraderie because the problems start on Thursday when the guys are putting the cars together," Force told NHRA.com. "It's not what's wrong on Friday morning when you made that run. The mistakes are usually made on Thursday. A lot of guys go to qualifying like it is a fun day. That is why we have team meetings. You can die during testing as easily as you can on race day."

"We look for people with similar approaches in the way they handle their jobs," Coil, whose job it is to put the team together, told RacingOne.com. "We usually spend about three days with potential hires, and if they don't fit in, they don't make the team. Some people may be very good at what they do, but disrupting what we have now would be doing the team more harm than good."

"There are creators and there are followers," Coil added. "The followers will win their share of races simply by preparing things the way they were taught to. And then there are guys that are brave enough and have been funded enough to get to the top of the heap by trying new things."

In 1997, John Force's team approach continued to provide positive results. Force opened the year right where he had left off in 1996, winning the first two events of the season. However,

All John Force ever wanted to be was a hero—on the football field, as a policeman, or as a drag racer. *Ron Lewis*

Drag racing's Superman, John Force won 7 of the year's first 11 events in 1999, setting speed (324.05 miles per hour) and elapsed time (4.788 seconds) marks along the way. *Jon Asher*

his relationship with Pontiac, with whom he'd been with since the beginning of 1995, continued to sour after the opener in Pomona, when Force's teammate, Tony Pedregon, showed up in a Ford.

After agreeing to a contract extension earlier in the season, Force wanted Pontiac, the 1996 NHRA Manufacturer of the Year, to step up its support of his second team car, so Tony's stunt wasn't appreciated. Then John showed up for the Gatornational weekend with the Pontiac emblem on his car, but by the final day of eliminations, the emblem was gone. By March, Pontiac ended the game altogether.

"Only after much deliberation must we inform our fans and team members, that effective immediately, John Force will no longer be with Team Pontiac," Firebird brand manager Jim Murray said in an issued statement. "It is our desire to move forward on a positive note."

"I think Pontiac was afraid Force was going to leave them anyway," Tony says. "So they decided to make the break before he did. I don't really think John was going to go anywhere. He was under contract."

Neither party gave details of the breakup. "Things like this happen," Pontiac spokesperson Jeff Romack said at the time. "Sometimes the less said about it the better."

Whatever the reason for the divorce, the result was an open door to the hottest driver in American motorsports, and drag racer Bob Tasca Sr., a successful Ford dealer from New England, seized the opportunity, introducing Force to executives of Ford Motor Company.

Bruce Cambern, worldwide head of Ford's racing program, commented on the situation at the time by saying, "He's obviously the biggest name in drag racing today. And when the opportunity presented itself, of course, we jumped right on it."

John Force had come full circle. He was back in a Mustang. Breaking in a new chassis, though, wasn't the only hurdle to Force's continued success. The 1997 season also brought a growing list of young contenders, all hungry for Force's title.

After struggling through years of partial schedules and small budgets, racing photographer-turned-driver Whit Bazemore picked up sponsorship from RJ Reynolds' Winston brand and joined the serious hunt for a championship. Although still not in the same financial ballpark as teams like Force, Joe Gibbs Racing, and Prudhomme's Snake Racing, Bazemore and crew chief Rob Flynn now had a $700,000 budget that improved their level of competitiveness.

In 1999, John donned the Superman paint scheme and won the inaugural Winston Showdown, a non-points event pitting Top Fuel against Funny Car. He defeated Top Fuelers Cristen Powell, Jim Head, Doug Kalitta, Cory McClenathan, and Bob Vandergriff to earn $200,000. *Jon Asher*

"I think John winning so easily [in 1996] embarrassed the rest of us a little," Bazemore said in *USA Today*. "It made a lot of teams work harder."

Through the years, Bazemore had been a true student of the game. Like Force, he studied winners from all walks of life, so he always paid very close attention to the way Force went about his business.

"I remember being a photographer at the U.S. Nationals in the early 1980s," Bazemore says. "I had been at the track late, and I was going back to my hotel around ten o'clock. There was a Wendy's restaurant on Crawfordsville Road, and Force's team was there doing a display. This was

race night or a day or two before, but they had come from the racetrack with their entire rig and set it up at this Wendy's. Force was a grease ball back then, a struggling racer, and struggling drag racers back then weren't the cleanest guys around. He was doing what you had to do . . . there are no free rides. Force was one of the guys who paid his dues early in his career."

"I love winning so much," Force once told *USA Today*. "Take it away and I'm nothing. Without the cheers of the crowd, I'm dead." *Jon Asher*

John's win-loss record was 61-11 in 1999 and his 81 career national victory total was just 4 wins shy of Pro Stock driver Bob Glidden's mark (85) as the most wins ever by a drag racer. *Jon Asher*

Along the way, John was surprised more of the drivers weren't trying to emulate his formula for success. Young drivers asked him why he was still running around doing appearances in front of Wal-Mart—after all, he was the best in the business. Why would the champ need to continue this kind of effort just to pick up a few bucks? Force's response was, "They just don't understand that it's all this running around that pays for everything we need to be the best. There must be something about young and stupid that goes together."

Bazemore, however, was the exception, knowing early on that Force had the proper approach to his career. "I lin aolo good in the early days was to build his team," Bazemore says. "He made money, and he reinvested it in his operation. There were other guys in that same position that didn't reinvest in their business, they did not give their cars everything they needed, and they're not out there anymore. That's one of the big lessons I learned from John. Reinvest in your team and business, and continue to grow."

"That's the thing that impresses me most about Force—his ability as a car owner," Bazemore adds. "He may not be a businessman in the strictest sense of the word, but he has the street smarts and the common sense to do what you have to do to be successful. I think at the end of his career that will be seen as one of the biggest reasons behind the success that he has had for so long."

John and two of his fiercest rivals, Whit Bazemore (left) and Al
Hofmann (right). Very rarely are all three of these men smiling at the
same time. *Jon Asher*

John collected his ninth Funny Car title in 1999 and was named one of
the top 50 drivers of the century by ESPN. *Carol Johnson*

In addition to the up-and-coming Bazemore, Force also had a formidable pair of rookies ready to take him on in 1997. Prudhomme had hired Ron Capps, the same Capps who Force had been considering to pilot the ride that eventually went to Tony Pedregon. And two-time Top Alcohol Funny Car champion Randy Anderson, a second-generation driver from California, was an instant contender after securing the Parts America sponsorship away from Hofmann.

By the second half of the 1997 season, all three young drivers were making their presence felt, putting increased pressure on John Force and his team. Bazemore won three events, including the U.S. Nationals. He also became the eighth member of the Castrol 4-Second Club and set the NHRA Funny Car speed record with a run of 313.04 miles per hour at the Slick 50 Nationals in March. Capps, after a slow start, picked up a pair of victories and the NHRA's Road to the Future Award, given annually to the driver who has the most promise in drag racing. Randy Anderson—the son of three-time Winston Top Alcohol Funny Car champion Brad Anderson—got off to the quickest start of all, earning Force's immediate attention. He won two of the first seven races he ran in the nitro division, stunning Force in the final round at the Fram Nationals in Atlanta after Force waited for him at the starting line. Repairing a cracked crankshaft caused Anderson's team to be slow to the line, but Force insisted they wait for the rookie.

"John could have raced without me, and he could have won," Anderson told *USA Today.* "They kept telling him to run a single, but he refused to run without me. That just shows how much class he has and why he is such a great ambassador for our sport."

Anderson later became the ninth member of the Castrol 4-Second Club and recorded top speeds at five national events, tying him with Force.

If Force was truly worried about the latest crop of young guns, he wasn't letting on to the media. "People ask me if I am worried about Randy Anderson," he said in a 1997 interview. "I say, 'When he gets his fifth championship, I'll be worried about him.'"

John finished the season with six wins in 10 final rounds, leading the points race all year. Though not in the dominant fashion he had displayed in 1996, he earned an unprecedented seventh

John and Austin closed out the millennium with championship No. 9 and a lot to talk about for the next millennium. At home, John's 16-year-old daughter Ashley was getting driving lessons at Frank Hawley's drag racing school. *Carol Johnson*

In 1999, John was the No. 1 qualifier nine times, posting low elapsed times at 15 events and top speed marks 12 times. *Jeff Burk*

Winston Funny Car Championship. And on the final pass of the final event of the season, teammate Tony Pedregon beat the boss in the Winston Finals to edge Bazemore for second in the points race. Capps finished fifth and Anderson sixth.

"You can take different approaches when you are racing against Force," Bazemore says. "You can think that he is just another guy, and their team is nothing special, just another competitor, or there are other times that you think, *This is John Force's team and John himself, and this is the six-time champion.* . . . You have to change your approach a little when you race him. I've done it different ways, and you'd like to think they are just another car. You have to make him a normal person, like he is no different than any of us, and at the end of the day, he isn't. They're just really good, and they don't make mistakes that often."

In 1998, it looked more and more like the field was catching up to Force and Coil. Force didn't win an event until the Mopar Nationals in Englishtown, the eighth stop on the NHRA tour, where he set an NHRA speed record of 323.89 miles per hour. The run marked the first time a Funny Car had broken the 320 barrier and was 8 miles per hour faster than the record coming into the season.

The team, however, followed the record-breaking performance with three first-round exits in the next five events. So at the U.S. Nationals on Labor Day weekend, John Force found himself in unfamiliar territory. Traditionally well ahead in points this late in the season, Force was trailing Capps heading into the sport's most prestigious event.

"I was starting to worry that I was running out of steam, and I was too stupid to know it," John, then 49, said in an interview for *National Speed Sport News*. "But the fans keep cheering for me, and they don't care how old I am. They just want to see that hot rod go down the track."

John and company show off an issue of *Hot Rod* magazine with the Force machine on the cover. In drag racing, the cars are the stars.
Jon Asher

Despite struggling early at Indy, Force and Coil came through on race day, mowing through the field en route to a final-round matchup with Anderson, whom Force defeated for just his second victory of the season. As a result, Force regained the points lead. However, the 1998 season would only become more challenging for the team.

Expecting to unveil a new chassis designed by the NASCAR experts at Roush Racing before the end of the season, John was loaded with confidence as he faced the remainder of the schedule. But after protests by other drivers and officials from Chevrolet, whose cars were second and third in points at the time, the NHRA rescinded its approval, postponing the new car's debut until the 1999 season.

"NHRA has the responsibility of maintaining the highest level of competition among its participating race teams," NHRA vice president Graham Light told *USA Today*. "Competition for the Winston Championship in both the Top Fuel and Funny Car categories is the closest in history. Implementation of any rule change which could have any negative impact upon that close competition is not in the best interest of the sport. As a result, implementation of the previously approved Funny Car body modification rule has been postponed until January 1, 1999."

Force's competitors agreed. "I think the world of John, and I understand his burning desire to win," Chuck Etchells said at the time. "But that's why we have a sanctioning body. A few teams could keep up with this change, but low-budget teams would be dead in the water."

Force, however, was furious. After using every profanity in the book at least three times, Force settled on this response with a reporter: "They can take all four wheels off my car and tie me up, but we are still going to keep going after [the championship]. Everyone still has to race us."

John and Austin have collected more "Wallys" and more NHRA championships than any other duo in the sport's history.
Jon Asher

Some of the drivers realized they were in trouble, as even Ron Capps talked of the mistake behind waking the sleeping giant. "John is the biggest thing in drag racing for a reason," Capps said. "I came out saying we wanted to beat John and win the whole thing. I was humbled very quickly."

"John works better under pressure," Tony Pedregon explains. "When any competitor ever got close, there was always a psychology he used. He wanted to know about everyone. That's the way he is wired.

"He goes into a panic and calls a team meeting, says it's going to last ten minutes, and it lasts an hour and ten minutes. But what he would do was bring everyone together, and that would make everyone pay closer attention and over the next race or two, and we'd get that lead back. John has become so accustomed to winning and understands it so well that he doesn't want to leave a whole lot out on the table. Anytime John has been threatened by someone coming in and trying to take something he has enjoyed for so long, that is probably when he is more focused and more lethal than any other time. Wherever he came from, he learned how to fight. John is always up for a fight."

Despite winning only one more time in 1998, Force's nine final-round appearances were enough to carry him into the Winston Finals with the points lead over Ron Capps. After the rookie fell in the first round at Pomona and Force defeated Dean Skuza in his match, Force had secured his eighth Funny Car title, surpassing championship marks set by racing greats Richard Petty and Dale Earnhardt in NASCAR. Capps finished second, but the other young guns who came in with their sights set on dethroning the king struggled. Bazemore, with new sponsor Kendall, finished fifth, and Anderson was a non-factor, as his Parts America sponsorship dried up.

"This one was the toughest ever," Force said after winning his record-setting title. "It doesn't matter how long you've been doing this. Before the first qualifying run, my knees were knocking, and I've been in the business for twenty-five years. I'm just going to take two weeks and spend some time with my kids. I just want to wake up in the morning and not feel sick to my stomach wondering if I am going to lose this thing."

After a few months off, Force, Coil, Bernie Fedderly, Tony Pedregon, and John Medlen returned to the track with a purpose in 1999. With their new Roush-designed chassis now legal, the team set out to reclaim its dominance in the Funny Car category. John jumped out to a commanding lead, winning seven of the year's first 11 races, setting speed (324.05 miles per hour) and E.T. records (4.788 seconds) along the way.

Pedregon's simple explanation for the team's success: They want it more than anyone else out there. "John's work ethic still comes through in everything he does," he says. "John's team is one of the first there in the morning, and ninety-eight percent of the time, they are going to be one of the last teams to leave. It's just another aspect of the winning formula that John has been able to maintain."

"I love winning so much," Force told *USA Today.* "Take it away, and I'm nothing. Without the cheers of the crowd, I'm dead."

In that same article, Force explained the extremes to which his desires take him. "Fear motivates you," John said. "I can't even enjoy going to the movies anymore because I'm thinking, 'What if my opponent learns what I've learned?' I know the Japanese lady at the doughnut shop and the guy at the movie theater. They are the only friends I have outside of drag racing. That's my world, along with my kids. My dog doesn't even know me."

En route to his ninth Winston Championship, John Force took on the entire nitro division as the NHRA experimented with a new format in the inaugural Winston Showdown, an event pitting Top Fuel cars against Funny Cars in a non-points fan fest. In typical Force fashion, John was all about winning, as he defeated Top Fuel drivers Cristen Powell, Jim Head, Doug Kalitta, Cory McClenathan, and Bob Vandergriff, earning $200,000. To top it all off, Force was named one of the top 50 drivers of the century by ESPN.

At home, he gave daughter Ashley drag racing lessons at Frank Hawley's drag racing school as a 16th birthday present. Apparently, it sparked an interest, as the cheerleader from Esperanza High School signed up for classes in auto shop and welding.

"You have to take an elective," she said on the team website. "I could have taken [home economics], which my mom said I should have because I don't know how to cook at all, [but] I thought auto shop would be more fun."

"I had just gotten my driver's license and Dad wouldn't even let me drive on the freeways," Ashley told *The Dallas Morning News.* "But I went to the driving school and got down the track at one hundred fifty miles per hour, I knew then it was what I wanted to do."

"I'm a typical father who always wanted his son to grow up and drive his race car," Force said on his website. "But I don't have any sons, so I always hoped one of my girls would have an interest."

Naturally, though, Force wasn't sure what he feared most: his daughter on fire at 300 miles per hour or the thought of her roaming the country with a crew full of car guys.

FORCE WRESTLES WITH HISTORY

"I'M CLAUSTROPHOBIC . . . AND YET
I GET IN THAT COCKPIT. I CAN'T
EXPLAIN IT, EXCEPT TO SAY THAT
CAR IS MY PERSONAL BUDDY."
— JOHN FORCE, *LOS ANGELES TIMES*

John won his 10th consecutive championship in 2000, earning double-
digit victories (11) for the fifth time in his career. *Jeff Burk*

When the 2000 testing sessions opened in Tucson, Force and company had two goals in their sights: a 10th NHRA Winston Funny Car title and five more national event wins.

Yes, John Force not only wanted to be the dominant driver of his era—he wanted to be considered the best drag racer of all time. But wherever he went, he was reminded of Pro Stock legend Bob Glidden's 85 national event victories. Though accumulated in a different class of hot rod, Glidden's mark was now within reach, as Force started 2000 with 81 trophies to his name.

Fastest at Pomona in testing with a run of 4.890 at 317.79 miles per hour in his Castrol Ford, John Force found that he had a new challenger to his crown. Jerry Toliver, in only his third season of NHRA competition, arrived at the Winternationals with heavy funding from the high-powered World Wrestling Federation and a veteran teammate, Jim Epler. Dale Armstrong, who tuned Kenny Bernstein to the title of "King of Speed," and clutch specialist Bob Brooks were handling the crew chief duties, and Toliver fired a shot over Force's bow with an impressive victory to start the season.

Force, however, may have been a bit distracted by activities in his pits. The NHRA had shortened the time teams had to service their cars between rounds, and Force's hospitality and pit area were, by far, the most popular sites for media and fans to gather and hang out. So John ended up employing security guards to keep people out of his area during the opening event, but the strong-armed tactic didn't go over too well with a group used to the all-access NHRA. In fact, by the end at Pomona, Force's police force was no longer in uniform and worked a little

John and teammate Tony Pedregon matched up on numerous occasions in 2000. Although the two appeared to race straight up in early season events, questions about "team orders" always lingered. *Jon Asher*

John's lucrative deal with Action Collectibles makes for an unending parade of special paint schemes. *Jon Asher*

harder to keep a low profile. The champion, always keenly aware of his relationship with both the media and the fans, worked tirelessly to maintain it.

"Whenever there is a hint that fans are upset at him, he calls me to ask me to help him fix it, to get his side of the story out to the people, so they will still like him," says long-time *National Dragster* editor Phil Burgess. "I can't count the number of times he's called me to ask for help because he is really concerned."

With the security issue under control, Force turned his attention back to racing. At the Checker Schuck's Kragen Nationals in Phoenix, John collected his first win of the season and 82nd of his career by rolling past Johnny Gray, Scotty Cannon, and Toliver before defeating Ron Capps in the final. Now only three wins behind Bob Glidden, Force tried to keep things in perspective, downplaying the chase as much as possible.

"Yeah, I want to break it," Force said at the time. "I would like to have the record because everywhere you walk into, someone will say the winningest guy in all the sport is Bob Glidden. Maybe someone will say that about me and maybe they won't, but I'm going to keep trying."

John takes only a brief second to catch his breath before seeking out the TV cameras and returning to the throng of fans waiting at his pit area. *Jeff Burk*

John spends more time "working the ropes" than any other NHRA drag racer. *Jon Asher*

With all eyes on Force's run for the record, a few still managed to notice that John was now bringing a third Funny Car to the track, a black and orange Mustang with "Aero Experimental" on it. Immediately, speculation began on who would pilot the third entry, with names like Gary Ormsby Jr. and Tommy Johnson Jr. high on the list.

In reality, though, only one car mattered. At the Gatornationals, Jerry Toliver proved he wasn't going away easily, knocking off Capps to win at Gainesville and taking the top spot in the points race.

"We want to stay ahead in the points lead and go wire to wire," Toliver, the nephew of drag racing greats Jack and Art Chrisman, said after the race. "This serves notice that this team is for real, that Pomona wasn't a fluke. I know we are going to have to fight for this thing. It's not going to be easy. John's going to be tough, but I think we are ready for him."

Again, Force showed signs of vulnerability a few weeks later in Houston. At the O'Reilly Nationals in mid-April, he was defeated in the first round by the No. 16 qualifier, Bob Gilbertson.

In 2000, John faced a new challenger to his Funny Car throne and to his dominance in souvenir sales. Jerry Toliver, with backing from the popular World Wrestling Federation, was ready for a Texas cage match against the multichampion. *Jon Asher*

John disappears into his comfort zone. *Ron Lewis*

"WE HAD 100,000 PEOPLE OUT AT POMONA AND 99,000 WERE AT MY ROPES. I SIGNED FROM EIGHT IN THE MORNING INTO THE NIGHT, AND I WAS EXHAUSTED. THEY ASK ME HOW I CAN DO WHAT I DO WITH A DRAGSTER. THAT [STUFF] IS EASY. THAT PART'S LIKE SEX. IT ONLY TAKES FIVE SECONDS."

— LOS ANGELES TIMES

A quality pre-run burnout spins the rear wheels to heat and clean the tires, allowing for more traction during the run. *Jeff Burk*

NHRA Funny Cars burn nitromethane, a fuel produced specifically for drag racing. It's the result of a chemical reaction between nitric acid and propane.
Ron Lewis

The team had replaced a newly fitted intake manifold after earning the top qualifying spot with a run of 4.839 at 319.98 miles per hour, and the Castrol hot rod dropped a cylinder, giving Gilbertson the upset win. It marked the end of an 81-race streak of first-round victories for John.

To make matters worse, Toliver made it to the final round and built on his early season points advantage. Not only was the newcomer doing well on the track, but his popular WWF merchandise was giving the Force selling machine a run for its money. Like Force, Toliver seemed to understand the business side of racing.

"I have the business sense to look at things from a different angle," Toliver told *USA Today.* "There is a changing of the guard going on in drag racing. It's not just competition anymore. It's entertainment."

At Richmond, Force got back on track with a tire-smoking win over Ron Capps, after defeating Gilbertson, Al Hofmann, and Scotty Cannon in eliminations. "That just shows what luck can do," Force said after the race. "The car was rattling so hard in the seat that I lost my vision. When I came around, all I could see was the 'U.S. Tobacco' [Capps' sponsor]. I actually thought he had lifted because I had crossed the centerline. But I didn't, and it turned out that he was having the same problem that I was." The win tightened the points battle, lifting Force from fourth to second, just 69 points behind Toliver.

The early season battle with a new foe brought out vintage Force gamesmanship. "We did gain some ground on Toliver's team," Force said after the win. "They'd better get ready for Atlanta because we are going to continue to stay after it and prove what we can do."

John celebrates another win. In 2000, Force broke Pro Stock driver Bob Glidden's career victory record of 85 NHRA national event wins. *Jeff Burk*

The head games appeared to have an effect on Toliver and Armstrong, as they began playing a game of musical cars. At the Southern Nationals in Atlanta, the team switched to a generic black Pontiac chassis, replacing the WWF-painted Camaro, as it was committed to neither manufacturer. Force followed up on his warning, driving past Gilbertson, WWF teammates Toliver and Epler, and Capps en route to his 84th career victory and trimming Toliver's points advantage to 30. All the while, Force continued to push Toliver's buttons.

"It was great racing today," Force said after the event. "Toliver is doing the talk of the WWF. It's a gimmick to create excitement. In the WWF, they yell and scream and throw each other off stages, and beat up their moms and dads. It's just what they do, but this is drag racing. Sometimes, if you hype too much, it can bite you."

John also reminded everyone that his business was still going strong when Action Collectibles unveiled a special paint scheme—and money-making die cast—celebrating Force's quest for a 10th title and his colorful history in the sport. Bringing back the *Brute Force* nickname and using a lightning bolt fist that first adorned Force's Monza in 1977, the new black car with "9-Time Champion" painted on the side was a hit with the fans.

A rainout at Englishtown forced Force to wait for the Castrol Nationals in Texas for his first run at tying Glidden's long-standing mark. In round one, he dispatched longtime rival

Castrol's "Drive Hard" marketing campaign was the perfect match for John Force and his approach to racing and to life. *Jon Asher*

Al Hofmann. In round two, he knocked off teenager Cristen Powell, but a blower explosion at the finish line forced him into a backup body for a semifinal matchup with Capps. Yet Force defeated Capps, creating an all-Castrol final at his sponsor's event, as teammate Pedregon also had worked his way through the field for the final-round matchup. When Tony lost traction right from the start, John found himself tied with Glidden at 85 and on top in the points race by 33 over Toliver.

"I'm happy to have it over with," Force said after his third consecutive win of the season. "It's kind of hard to claim a victory and jump up and down 'cause I never raced Bob Glidden in my life. Now, my deal is to stay focused and do everything I've done for the last ten years."

Although John downplayed the achievement publicly, his peers were quick to weigh in on the accomplishment.

"I'll tell you, eighty-five victories is just an unbelievable achievement," three-time Top Fuel champion Gary Scelzi said after Force reached the mark. "I can't imagine winning eighty-five races in one of the toughest divisions in drag racing. The combination of John Force and Austin Coil is just awesome. Just think of where John would be if he'd been with Coil since the beginning. We might be talking about John going for a hundred wins now instead of eighty-six.

"I know there are still a lot of Bob Glidden fans out there, so I've got to be careful when I say this, but I think Force's eighty-five wins are more impressive. Now, maybe that's because I'm a nitro guy, but to do what he's done in a 320-mile-an-hour hot rod, that's something. My hat's off to Force."

Even Force's hero, Don Prudhomme, acknowledged John's position in the sport. "I want to see him win," Prudhomme said in *Performance Trends*. "He puts everything into it. People boo [NASCAR driver Jeff Gordon], and they hated me when I won, but John seems to keep winning,

(Continued on page 129)

John puts in the time between rounds to get his car just right for competition. *Ron Lewis*

"WHEN I AM UP THERE IN THAT BED, I'M AFRAID THAT SOMEONE IS STEALING MY FAME OR STEALING MY SPONSORS, OR WINNING A RACE BECAUSE I AIN'T THERE."
— JOHN FORCE, *LOS ANGELES TIMES*

Masters of their craft—Austin Coil (left) and John Force (seated).
Ron Lewis

The addition of crew chief John Medlen (right) continued to serve John's quest for constant improvement and domination. Medlen's specialties are design and fabrication.
Ron Lewis

John's operation now runs on the best parts in the business—a far cry from the days when he was chased away from every trash can and trailer, scrounging for used and discarded parts. *Jon Asher*

and people love him. John Force will go down in history as one of the guys who did a lot for the sport, more so than [Don] Garlits or [Shirley] Muldowney."

Force wasted no time in passing Glidden, defeating John Lawson, Pedregon, and Capps before facing down Toliver in the final of the Prestone Route 66 Nationals in Chicago. Toliver set a career-best mark of 4.831 at 314.53 miles per hour in his semifinal win over Del Worsham, and beat Force off the line in the final, but Force took the win—4.842 at 318.09 to Toliver's 4.932 at 312.64. Toliver again alternated Pontiac and Camaro bodies during the event, finishing in the Camaro. And while Toliver's team was looking for an aero edge, Force was working on plans of his own, preparing to bring out yet another Roush-designed chassis exclusive to him and his team.

John's special edition "Driver of the Year" car takes to the track in 1997. *Ron Lewis*

NHRA chief starter Rick Stewart (right) is only the second person to hold that position in NHRA history, replacing Buster Couch. He's pushed the button for nearly all of John Force's victories. *Jeff Burk*

When John's new frames showed up in mid-June, one painted and one unpainted, they didn't exactly set the track in Columbus, Ohio, on fire. Nearly bumped from the field during final qualifying at the Pontiac Excitement Nationals, Force settled for the No. 15 position, his worst in 130 events, and lost to Toliver in the first round, giving his new rival an 11-point advantage in the points race. Toliver extended his points lead to 54 at the midpoint of the season, winning his third national event—the Sears Craftsman Nationals in St. Louis—knocking off Force in the semis before beating Dean Skuza in the final.

"Any time you can beat John, it's good," Toliver said at the time. "You've beaten the best in the business."

Still tinkering with the new Ford body in Denver, Coil and Bernie Fedderly began to get things figured out, sending John on a tear through the remainder of the NHRA Western Swing. The team cut Toliver's lead to 32, defeating him in the semifinals at Seattle's Northwest Nationals, before winning the event by knocking off Frank Pedregon.

"They've got a smart team over there at WWF," Force, who also went on a crash diet to ensure he was physically up for the season-long fight, said after the event. "They're consistent. Fortunately, we were able to beat them today. It's going to be a real dogfight for the championship."

At Sonoma, however, the WWF brain trust failed, as Toliver gave up his points lead in the worst possible way—by not qualifying for the Fram Autolite Nationals. All John needed to do to take the lead was win two rounds of racing. He did much more, though, winning his seventh event of the season, when teammate Tony Pedregon fouled in the final. Despite the chorus of cries that Pedregon was rolling over for Force (he had lost 10 of 14 races to the boss), Force once again was the championship points leader.

"Our game plan is to whip the WWF team," Force said at the time. "I love Jerry and I felt real bad for him when he didn't qualify . . . but we want to beat him this year for the Winston Championship. That's what we are after."

John has a special relationship with his race cars, even if they are only small-scale models of the real thing. *Jon Asher*

Although the race only lasts a few seconds, the G-forces the body endures and the pressure to win or go home take their toll. *Jon Asher*

Force's advantage in the event had come from his experience driving on marginal tracks as a young driver, an endeavor Coil had orchestrated so that John could learn how to drive when the tracks weren't in top condition. Toliver had not had the same training.

"I'm not going to lay it off because everyone had the same field to play on," Toliver told *National Speed Sport News.* "But we are up against the three worst tracks on the circuit. Basically, what we are doing is trying to back these cars off so we can make it down the track."

Toliver's struggles continued in Brainerd, where he qualified No. 15 in yet another new frame and lost in the first round to Del Worsham. Force went on to win, defeating Toliver's teammate, Epler, in the final round. Team Force rolled out of Brainerd with a 160-point lead, having outscored Toliver and crew by 212 points since Seattle. Memories of the 1992 collapse and eventual loss to Cruz Pedregon kept John from getting too excited about the prospects of a 10th title.

"We went into test mode, and Cruz won five races in a row while I couldn't get past the first round without tripping over my roof," Force reminded everyone.

John's special 11-time champion Mustang. *Jon Asher*

At the 46th U.S. Nationals, neither Force nor Toliver enjoyed center stage in drag racing's premier event, as John went out in the second round and Jerry exited in the first. Force, however, did collect $100,000 for winning the Big Bud Shootout, and the extra round allowed him to tack a few more points onto his lead before everyone returned to New Jersey for the conclusion of the rain-delayed Spring Nationals.

When Force eliminated Toliver, the WWF tried in desperation to stop the bleeding, sending its entire crew to help Pedregon in his final-round matchup with Force. The move worked, as Pedregon won, but it proved to be an effort in futility for the latest challenger to Force's throne.

At Topeka, Force built his lead to 272 points with his 90th career victory, defeating both Toliver and Epler along the way.

"Force is out there and he's pretty much clinched it," Capps conceded after the event. "Mathematically, maybe not, but realistically, he has."

The reality of a 10th title came in Houston, on October 20 at the Matco Tools SuperNationals, when John clinched the championship. Then he added to his crown by winning the rescheduled O'Reilly Fall Nationals in Dallas by knocking off Toliver in the final with a run of 4.863 at 302.55 miles per hour to Toliver's 4.994 at 306.40. Another exclamation point came when Force won the final event of the year and signed a new five-year deal with Ford. The deal included a new convertible Jaguar XKR for the 10-time champion, and Toliver, Capps, and the rest of the field were forced to wait until next year for another shot at greatness.

FORCE RACING ENDURES MAJOR CHANGES

"I LIKE TO TALK. IT GETS ME IN TROUBLE A LOT, BUT I'M CONTINUALLY GOING AND I'VE LEARNED THAT EVEN IF I AM CAUGHT OFF GUARD, I TRY TO BE POSITIVE."

When John's driving days are done, not only will he be remembered as one of the best drivers in drag racing, but his reputation as a fierce and dedicated competitor will not fade away. *Jon Asher*

In 2001, John Force decided he wanted a third car in his racing stable, and he knew just who he wanted behind the wheel—his old friend Gary Densham. Densham, a veteran of years of match racing and modest attempts to compete at NHRA national events, had enjoyed a much quieter career path since the two shared racing adventures in Australia nearly 30 years earlier, but John felt the longtime driver was ready for the pressure and spotlight of being on Team Force.

"I hadn't really thought about Densham, but when John mentioned him, I knew he was the guy who could eliminate our problems," Tony Pedregon told NHRA.com. "He could handle the media, the PR, and he was well liked. That was important to John. Gary was someone that you didn't have any doubts about. When John mentioned him, he went right to the top of my list. He was a good pick."

The crowd comes to their feet anytime John is on the track. *Jon Asher*

Gary Densham claimed his first career NHRA national event victory in 2001 driving for John Force. Racing on a limited budget for much of his career, Densham had run more than 200 NHRA national events without a victory before teaming with his old friend. Force knew Gary had the talent, and with Force's unlimited resources, Densham went on to collect seven more NHRA victories, including one at the 2004 U.S. Nationals. *Ron Lewis*

John talks with drag racing legend Don Garlits. During the NHRA's 50th anniversary in 2001, Garlits and Force were named the top two drivers in the sport's history. *Jeff Burk*

"I view a driver as not only someone who can get into the car and negotiate it down the track, but someone that can also make an impact with the team," Pedregon continued. "Gary seems to be able to do that. There aren't a lot of guys who can actually make a difference."

Again, competitors complained Force was blocking the competition by adding a third car, but Densham did something to immediately silence the critics: He won. Having reached the finals only six times in 19 years on the NHRA circuit, he had never won an NHRA national event in 245 attempts. He won his first for John Force Racing at Memphis. He won his second at Dallas. Both came against his new boss. As he had done with Tony Pedregon years ago, Force demanded his old friend race him straight up, at least early in the season.

"If you could choreograph a race at almost three hundred twenty miles per hour, where the winning margin was about six-thousandths of a second, then you'd better be Siegfried & Roy," Densham said about his performance, which didn't surprise his old friend John.

"For Gary not to win in that many years, the pendulum had to start swinging his way," John said in the *Las Vegas Review-Journal.* "We always knew the talent he had. He was always kicking my butt at match races. A lot of people questioned the choice, but I knew he could drive a race car. He's probably been down more backwoods drag strips than anybody except maybe me and [Al] Hofmann. In this sport, there's no substitute for experience."

John with Top Fuel racer Chris Karamesines, whose colorful career spans six decades. If John stays behind the wheel as long as "The Greek," hitting the 200 win mark isn't out of the question. *Jeff Burk*

Later that year, John suffered a heartbreaking personal loss, when his mother, Betty Ruth, died at the age of 77 in October. "She was almost eighty years old, but she packed a hundred years into her life," Force said after her passing. "She was a big fan of drag racing, as responsible for getting me to this point as Austin Coil or Bernie Fedderly."

But he didn't let his grief take over his track performance, as he added yet another NHRA title that year, his 11th, and won a 12th in 2002, with teammates Tony Pedregon and Densham also finishing in the top 10 both years.

The 2003 season proved to be the most pivotal for John Force Racing. In the first four races, John found himself in unfamiliar territory, with a car that had seen many chassis and clutch changes.

In 2002, John won his 10th consecutive Funny Car title and the three John Force Racing cars combined to win 16 of the year's 23 events. *Jon Asher*

John won his 12th title in 2002 with teammates Tony Pedregon and Gary Densham both finishing in the top 10. *John Asher*

John earned his 100th career victory in 2002, second only to NASCAR legend Richard Petty for wins in all major motorsports. *Jon Asher*

As a result, the 12-time champ was outside the top 10 in points, with no sign of being able to climb back in. Six races into the season, John had been eliminated in the first or second round at every event.

As the season wore on, rumors of unrest at John Force Racing were starting to grow louder. In the midst of the points battle, Pedregon was talking to Force about potentially not returning in 2004. Sponsor pressures also meant Densham, more than likely, would be giving up his seat to a younger driver sooner rather than later.

The distractions and Force's struggles with the NHRA's new LED starting lights on the Christmas tree manifested themselves on the track, as Force tripped the red light at Englishtown, Topeka, Brainerd, and Pomona to close the season. Although he won three events and set a national record along the way, 2003 proved to be John's worst season since the late 1980s. For the first time in nearly 15 years, he did not hold his familiar spot atop the point standings.

"This is no different from the first ten years of my career, when I lost all the time," Force told *The Seattle Times*. "It has become expected that this team will just win. There have been twelve years of being good, and this year has just been average. We're not doing that bad. It is just that my other two cars are better."

Coil put things in perspective by saying, "It's not that winning feels so good. It's that losing feels so damn bad."

As the year came to a close, John sat uncomfortably in the middle of the pack and could only watch as Tony Pedregon battled Whit Bazemore for the title.

"Realistically, with Tony still three hundred twenty-six points ahead [of me], my job has changed," Force said after a win in Denver. "The last ten years, my job was to win the championship for my team and for my sponsors . . . but now my job is to beat Baze [Bazemore] and Worsham and [Ron] Capps and everyone else to help Tony win this title for Castrol Syntec. We've got three race cars over here, but this is one team, and when one of us wins the championship, we all win."

Despite the sponsor-speak, the joy of Pedregon's first championship and the frustration of Force's third-place finish could not coexist at John Force Racing. After the season, Pedregon made the difficult decision to walk away from his position as Force's No. 2, announcing he would team with his brother and longtime Force nemesis, Cruz, on a new two-car, family-run team.

For Tony, the decision wasn't an easy one. "It was tough for a couple of reasons," he said at the time. "I will always be indebted to John for the opportunity, and after spending the years with someone, building a relationship with someone for eight years, it's something that is difficult to walk away from. But I had just gotten to that point in my career. A lot of people thought because I won the championship, I was given an offer, but truthfully, this was something I was thinking about the year before. There was interest there, and a couple of offers came along years before, and I was starting to feel some of the challenges of driving for a multi-car team. Force was No. 1. Force was the priority. After four or five years, I understood my job and that all of the business decisions would not

In 2003, John felt all alone because he was out of the championship race for the first time since losing the title in 1992 and his team was in turmoil. *Jon Asher*

John struggled in 2003, getting eliminated in the first or second round in each of the season's first six events, leaving him well outside the top 10 in points. *Jon Asher*

always be beneficial to me. In fact, the decision to go out on my own was the only business decision I ever made."

"Ultimately, I think it is what anyone would want to do," Pedregon continued. "I felt it was time to do it. When I won the championship, I felt like my job was done. I knew that if I walked away, we'd still be friends, and we are. Every time I see him, I tell him I miss him—right up until the time we have to race each other. I never thought I would race without him. Sometimes I miss it, and sometimes I don't, but I always miss John."

Force even tried to sweeten the pot in an attempt to keep Pedregon, but Pedregon wanted control over his own destiny. "I don't know if you'd call it an offer or a counteroffer, but he offered me a long-term contract, signing bonus, and [salary] increase," Tony told *National Dragster*. "But, really, I felt that should have been there anyway because we won the championship, and I always went above and beyond what I felt the expectations were. It was something that I considered, and my decision came right down to the end, but the fact that I could control everything that I do was more appealing."

Publicly, John put the best spin on the loss of his No. 2, letting him out of his contract a few weeks early.

"Tony's been a great teammate," he told *Drag Racing Online*. "We wish him the best except, of course, when he pulls alongside one of our Fords. I don't know exactly what he's doing, but I

It would be Force's longtime No. 2, Tony Pedregon, who would be the dominant driver in 2003. Tony established career bests for wins (8), No. 1 qualifiers (8), elapsed time (4.721 seconds), and speed (326.79 miles per hour). *Jon Asher*

THE GOSPEL ACCORDING TO JOHN

"THAT'S THE PROBLEM WITH TOO MANY SUPERSTARS. THEY GET TOO MUCH MONEY, TOO MANY FERRARIS, AND THEY FORGET WHY THEY CAME. THEY FORGOT WHAT MADE THEM A STAR AND THE PEOPLE WHO GOT THEM THERE AND THE FANS WHO GOT THEM THERE, AND THAT'S WHAT I DON'T WANT TO LOSE."

— *LOS ANGELES TIMES*

John had mixed emotions about Tony winning the 2003 title. The trophy was a team trophy, but Pedregon was leaving and Force wasn't the champ. *Ron Lewis*

know it's always been his dream to race with his brother Cruz, and I know better than anyone else how important it is to follow your dream."

"We've had eight years together and I've seen him grow up," Force added. "I have a lot of mixed emotions about seeing him go. I would have liked for him to stay, and the door's still open for him. But at the same time, I'm proud that we were able to put him in a position, in a really tough economy, where he could go out and find his own deal."

Occasionally, though, other feelings about the relationship appeared in the press. "As much as I make statements like Tony was like my kid, the truth is I hardly knew Tony Pedregon," Force told *The Arizona Republic*. "I've read some things that Tony said, like I was holding him back. Well, I did. It was my team and my deal. It was about me. But as it evolved, it became time to be about Tony, too."

Pedregon, however, felt pushed into the decision to leave. "During the whole process, I was very honest with John, and I told him long before I made any decision that it was something I was considering," he said in the *Las Vegas Sun*. "I think John thought it was a bluff until he really gave me an ultimatum and said, 'You need to make a decision,' and I wasn't prepared to make a decision.

"To be fair to him, I called him and told him that if I'm going to be given an ultimatum, I won't be signing a contract. Of course, John . . . maybe sometimes you get so caught up in the business aspect of it, but I kind of felt like John's response was that he would find another driver, and that kind of hurt my feelings. Really, at that point, there was no turning back for me. I hadn't made any decision yet, but because I'm an honest person, I felt that I owed it to John to tell him even when I was just thinking about it."

Coming off one of the worst seasons of his career and his young lieutenant turning in his keys, John Force was at a crossroads and the racing world was quietly wondering if it was witnessing the end of a dynasty—or at the very least, a chink in the coat of Force's armor that once seemed impenetrable.

"The more you've won, the more embarrassing it is to lose," Coil said in *National Dragster*. "You are expected to win, you have the resources to win, and if you stop winning, people are going to say that you are too old to care anymore. But right now, the handwriting is not on the wall."

Coil also admitted that as the operation grew, so did the challenges of running the organization. "Every time you add another car, you add another ten people or so to the organization," he said on the team's website. "To have ten people who can work together is tough. To have twenty people who can work together is tougher. To have thirty people who can work together is really tough.

After losing the title to departing teammate Tony Pedregon in 2003, Force was more determined than ever to regain his title, labeling his 2004 campaign "The Redemption Tour." *Jeff Burk*

Now, I think we have forty-three who are on the road with us on a regular basis. But we've been pretty fortunate with the guys who have come along. You lose a few crew guys every year, but that's just part of the game. We train a few more and life goes on. The key guys are still here, and that's what matters."

Frustrated and hurt with the turmoil in his stable, John Force still showed no signs of quitting, instead spending time rebuilding John Force Racing for the 2004 season—a year he christened "The Redemption Tour."

"There will be a day, no doubt, when Force gets up in the morning and he decides he doesn't want to drive anymore," Coil said at the time. "It happened to [Kenny] Bernstein. He got up and said it was going to be his last year. [Don] Prudhomme did that, too. But you know what? When we are out here, it is very obvious to me that Force gets more fun out of driving that car than anything else he does in his life. I don't think he is anywhere near thinking about quitting yet. I wouldn't be surprised if he was driving ten years from now."

With the money and the pedigree to sign nearly any driver he wanted to replace Tony Pedregon, John made a short, half-hearted attempt to sign three-time NHRA Top Fuel champion Gary Scelzi. Mike Dunn, working in the NHRA television booth for ESPN after his Top Fuel ride with longtime friend and team owner Darrell Gwynn evaporated, also inquired about the ride.

"I tried to get myself in that seat," Dunn says. "I knew that would be a top-rate ride obviously—it had just won the championship. After talking with John, however, I felt that John wanted to put a young driver in the car. It's what he wanted to do, but he knew it would be a hard sell with his sponsors. He had a list of three or four veteran drivers in case he couldn't sell a younger driver, and I was number three or four, so I knew I didn't have a shot at it because I was too far down the food chain."

Scelzi, however, was higher on the list. His move from Top Fuel to Funny Car in 2002 was unspectacular at best, but multi-team owner Don Schumacher, determined to put together a program that would truly challenge Force, also was courting the gregarious Fresno, California,

John "helped older cars feel young again" by reloading the John Force Racing stable with unknowns Eric Medlen and Robert Hight, while John's daughter Ashley began working her way up the ranks. *Ron Lewis*

driver. Ultimately, Force wasn't willing to give Scelzi the pay he was looking for, and even more than that, he wasn't convinced a guy wearing three championship rings would be willing to race for anything less than a title shot.

Scelzi went with Schumacher, and Force convinced his sponsors to let him keep the job in-house, handing the keys to former high school rodeo champion Eric Medlen, son of longtime Force employee John Medlen, crew chief for the car Eric would be driving. Shaken by Pedregon's departure, John wanted someone loyal to the program.

"We talked to a lot of very talented drivers," Force said in a press release. "But, bottom line, we had an opportunity to give a young driver a chance and, after talking to all my crew chiefs, that's what we decided to do. Eric has been here for the last eight years. He knows our routine. He knows what we expect. He tested in my car [the Castrol GTX High Mileage Ford Mustang] after Vegas [last October], and that really is what told us that he had the potential to do the job."

Gary Densham also had planned to leave at the end of 2003, but Force convinced his friend to stay on and help the team through the turmoil.

Eric Medlen was an eight-year crew member and son of crew chief John Medlen. *Jon Asher*

Team Force is not hard to spot. They always are together . . . and usually celebrating. *Ron Lewis*

John and his team get ready in the staging lanes before taking to the track. *Jon Asher*

"Gary and I had a parting of the ways at the end of the year," Force explained to *National Dragster.* "Gary wanted to build his own program for his son, Steven, but with all of the problems that I had, I needed some experience in my camp, and let me tell you, he made me humble. It wasn't an easy sell to get him back. We've signed a four-year deal with the Automobile Club of Southern California, and Gary has agreed to give me one more year, and I thank him for that."

With an obvious new emphasis on keeping it all in the family, Force also began preparing daughter Ashley for her move up the racing ladder, turning her over to veteran driver developers and car owners Jerry Darien and Ken Meadows. Ashley graduated from Cal State Fullerton in 2003 with a degree in communications and an unofficial minor in racing, having split study efforts between college and seat time behind the wheel of a Super Comp dragster. Ashley's unexpected growing interest in racing put her on common ground with her father for the first time in their lives. But if there is any bitterness surrounding the years lost due to John's grueling schedule, the younger Force doesn't let it show.

"He was on the road a lot, but it had to be the focus of his life for him to get to where he is today," Ashley said in an interview with *The Dallas Morning News.* "When he was home, it couldn't have been easy having all daughters. Sometimes, we would go out to dinner, my sisters and I would talk about cheerleading and dancing. Dad would talk about racing. Neither of us knew what the other was saying.

"Now, Dad and I have common ground to talk about, but he still sees me as a teenager sometimes. After a race I might go out somewhere and he says, 'Wait a minute. Shouldn't I give

Bernie Fedderly (left) has been with John since midway through the 1992 season and is one of only two crew chiefs to win a championship in both Top Fuel and Funny Car racing. *Jon Asher*

you some kind of curfew?' Mom just laughs at that. She tells him to stick to the same plan they've always had, which is leaving the discipline decisions to her."

"When our youngest were babies, John would be gone so long racing that when he came home and tried to hold them, they'd get scared at who this strange man was and burst into tears," wife and mom Laurie told *USA Today*. "He can't tell you the date of the kids' birthdays or our wedding anniversary, but he can tell you around the time of which race they fell. He can't even tell you the kids' middle names. That's why I named them A, B, and C [Ashley, Brittany, and Courtney]. It makes it easier for him to remember."

"I really didn't know Ashley until now," John said in one interview. "My wife said the kids had a routine whenever I was coming home. I would drive up and Laurie would say, 'Dad's here,' and all the kids would run to the TV set to see me. They knew me through ESPN."

"You know what I missed in my life? I missed Elvis—that was a bummer. I missed being the first Funny Car in the [four-second range], and I missed my children," Force said in the *Las Vegas Review-Journal*. "Those are the three things I can never fix in my lifetime. And my children are the most important, and I'll spend the next fifty years trying to fix that."

Although a little less talkative than her dad, Ashley quickly lined up a powerful sponsor as a young driver. Mattel, famous for its work in the 1970s Hot Wheels marketing of "The Snake" and

Force crew chief Austin Coil with his trademark toothpick. *Jon Asher*

"The Mongoose" rivalry between Prudhomme and Tom McEwen, decided to back her big time—even producing an Ashley Force doll, complete with fire suit. Ford Motor Company wanted in on the act as well, making no secret of its plan to elevate women racers in all disciplines, including drag racing.

"Our racing products—to the best extent possible—ought to mirror our customers," Dan Davis, Ford's director of racing technology, said in *USA Today.*

And Ashley will learn to give those sponsors a great return on their investment from one of the best teachers—her dad. "She has to learn the business," John Force said in a Q&A distributed by NHRA Communications. "I have always made that clear to her. She went by me one time and she didn't have her Ford hat on. She was going to meet with ESPN. I told her she wasn't doing Ford any good if she didn't have something with their logo on. She didn't have her uniform yet. She went right back and got it."

When it comes to working a crowd of fans, the soft-described shy girl knows she will never come close to being the ONE-man, three-ring circus her father is.

"I don't talk as much as him, but who does?" Ashley explained to the *Dallas Morning News.* "Basically, I am a little more sane."

"The media attention was one of the toughest things to deal with," she said in *Hot Rod.* "I remember when they came to film my dad when I was eight. I was terrified. But when I started racing in Super Comp, I remember the first day I had a newspaper set up to interview me. It's

The next generation of Force, Ashley *(above and right)* **is being brought through the ranks at a cautious pace by her father. In 2004, John and Ashley both won their classes at the season-ending NHRA event, sharing the podium as the first father-daughter event winners in NHRA history.** *Ron Lewis/John Asher*

something you get used to. It's a lot more fun now. And you realize that they're just interested in telling your story."

As the 2004 season continued, John kept a close watch over Ashley but trusted her training to Darien and Meadows, a tandem with a well-documented success rate. The team's alumni include Funny Car drivers Gary Scelzi and Frank Pedregon, as well as Top Fuel pilots Brandon Bernstein, Morgan Lucas, and Melanie Troxel.

"She still needs seat time," Force said at the time. "Anybody can drive a car from A to B when everything's perfect. The key is to be able to drive in trouble, and that's what she is learning

The smile returned to John's face in 2004. His five victories on the season upped his NHRA-record career total to 114 and gave him at least one victory for 18 consecutive seasons. *Jon Asher*

from Darien and Meadows. She's learning how to 'pedal' and how far she can drive it without getting in trouble. This is a serious race car. They're going faster in the alcohol cars than I was when I won my first Funny Car race. So I want her to get all the experience she can. She's got time. I didn't win my first race until I was thirty-seven."

Ashley didn't have to wait that long, as she scored the first win of her career at the prestigious 2004 U.S. Nationals, defeating Shelly Howard 5.32 to 5.38 in a historic all-female final. It marked only the third time in the sport's history that a woman had won the U.S. Nationals.

"It took me fifteen years to win there, and I think seven of those I was on fire," John said about his daughter's historic win.

Ashley then collected another national event win and three regional victories as the season progressed, but at the season-ending NHRA event in Pomona, her dad shared in the success as both he and Ashley won their classes at the Automobile Club of Southern California Finals, becoming the first father-daughter event winners in NHRA history. To boot, John's win against Del Worsham secured his 13th national championship and the redemption he had predicted all along.

"This is just a great weekend, an emotional weekend," he said in a post-race interview. "This was a look at the future of John Force Racing, a changing of the guard. When she won, I came to life. I don't think I could be any prouder. She is doing a job. I don't know where she got it. To have that composure and coolness. The pressure doesn't seem to affect her the way it affects me. It's been real scary with me with her. I have to get over it. As a father, it's tough to watch."

With his own place in racing history secure, now John is motivated by what he sees in Ashley. "She has a chance as a woman, like Shirley Muldowney, to do something to help build the sport to the next level."

The "Next Generation" movement continued at the end of 2004, when John announced that Gary Densham would be replaced by Force's son-in-law, Robert Hight [daughter Adria's husband], giving him a pair of unproven teammates.

"We all hate change, but we know it's inevitable," Force said at the time. "I have to give the companies that support me a ten- to twenty-year program."

"It's the changing of the guard," he added in a press release. "With Robert and before him Eric and my daughter Ashley, we're making a game plan to keep this race team on top long after I've taken my last ride."

"My main job the next six years is to win championships for Castrol, Ford, and the Auto Club," Force continued, "but my other job is to help train these kids. It's an exciting time for me, and I can't wait to get started."

In addition to his daughter and son-in-law, the other "kids" Force was referring to are his younger daughters, Brittany and Courtney, who both have Super Comp licenses.

So with a whole new generation of Force drivers making names for themselves, John's legacy will continue to grow even after he finally decides his driving days are done.

As for Force's place in the sport, NHRA founder Wally Parks doesn't hesitate to say John is one of the most impressive drivers ever. "He has combined skill, personality, and salesmanship to benefit himself and our sport," he says. "I hold him in very high esteem."

"John Force's impact on the sport has been, and continues to be, huge," Funny Car driver Mike Dunn says. "I know [the NHRA] wouldn't be where we are today without him. He's the working man's driver. He's one of the few guys that can win all those races and people still love him.

"His approach is different than that of most of the other team owners and drivers. He caters more to the fans. Some drivers won't do autograph sessions unless it is sponsor related. For the most part, John will stop and sign, even when he's running up to the staging area. He really loves the fans and he feeds off that."

Yet no one should let John's "dumb ol' truck driver" bit fool them. "John's obviously a pretty smart guy underneath all that farce he puts out," says drag racing legend Kenny Bernstein, the only team owner in motorsports to collect victories in three major series—NHRA, NASCAR, and Indy Car. "He kind of acts like he doesn't know what he is talking about, but he really does."

"It will be a great loss when John steps out of the seat," Bernstein adds. "You're not going to replace John Force right away. You look at our sport and there are a lot of young drivers coming up, but they haven't won enough yet and haven't established themselves day in and day out, year after year. That's what you have to do in this game."

As for Force behind the wheel of a Funny Car, well, who knows when that he'll decide he's ready to do something else full time. "When John decides to quit, then somebody else will have a shot at the championship," says friend and rival Al Hofmann. "As long as John Force is racing in that car, I believe he will be the champion. Even with Tony's deal, he had control over that and he let it happen. All the money went in the same kitty."

"He's the true American success story," Bob Fisher said in the *Las Vegas Review-Journal*. "He tried harder than anyone else to get where he is today. He went through a lot of people saying he wouldn't be anything."

Coil doesn't see his boss and good friend slowing down anytime soon. "As long as he is alive, he will be a team owner," Coil predicted in *National Dragster*. "He has the gift of being able to manage sponsors and gather money from everywhere to keep the organization going. Even when the economy is tough, he gets it done. So it isn't likely he is going to quit, whether his kids take over driving his cars at some point or whether he will have hired drivers. It doesn't matter; there will be a Force team for a long time."

"I've already heard it from people: 'He is going to lose focus because of his daughter and he is going to forget how to race,'" Force said in a Q&A for *NHRA.com*. "Let me tell those people something: I have more than twenty-five years of learning how to win. I know when you have to focus on winning and I know when you have to focus on your daughter. I just want to give my children some extra time that I never gave them before. But when it comes time to run my car, I'm there when it is time to warm it up, and I am there when it is time to race. Trust me . . . they are talking to a polished veteran with a clean medical report.

"But most important, I want to prove to my daughter that you never quit trying, and that is important to me. Even if your age has caught up to you, and I don't believe mine has, that you take whatever situation and you size up your finances, your talent, your ability, your age, your crew, your team. Through short hair, long hair, different kinds of music, crazy on the stage to calm on the stage, John Force is going to adapt."

Adapt yes, but truly change, never. Still based in Yorba Linda, less than 30 miles from the Bell Gardens trailer park he grew up in, Force remains most comfortable while on the move.

John Force where he always wants to be—at the center of attention.
Jon Asher

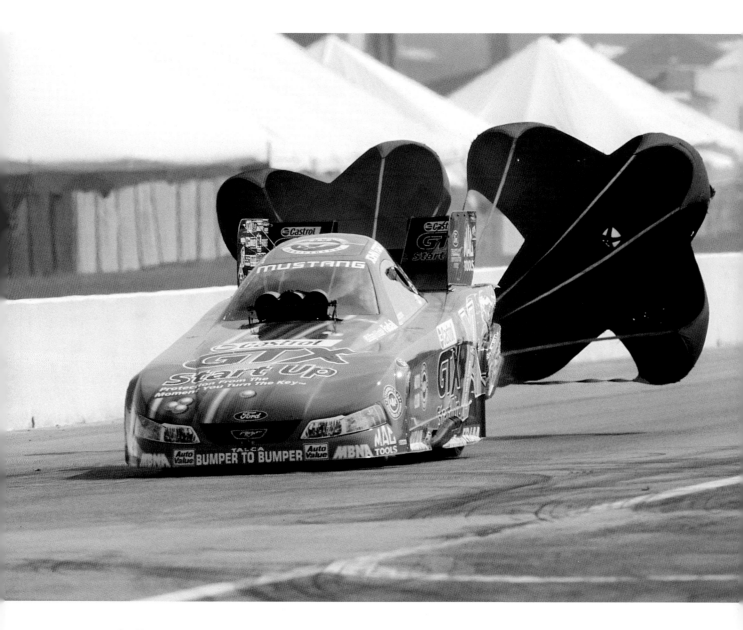

**Coil doesn't see his boss slowing down anytime soon: "As long as he is
alive, he will be a team owner," he says.** *Jon Asher*

Despite multiple real estate holdings, including a hillside home overlooking the childhood exis-
tence he left behind, Force spends much of his time in a new trailer park, made up of fancy
motor coaches and team haulers at each weekend's NHRA event. And though he now com-
mands infinitely more than the $1,600 appearance fees he hustled for in the early days, every
waking minute is still spent thinking of the next deal.

"At seventy-five, I am going to orchestrate my own wheelchair operation," Force said in one
interview. "I am going to pull all of the drivers out of retirement and I am going to allow the fans to
pay to push us around the pits. They can push Al Hofmann, John Force, and Don Prudhomme
around in the pits in the wheelchairs. At that age, I will still be figuring out how to make money."

APPENDIX

JOHN FORCE CAREER HIGHLIGHTS

- Winner of 10 consecutive NHRA Funny Car championships (1993–2002).
- Winningest driver in drag racing history with 119 tour victories (through October 2005).
- Winner of a record 13 series championships (1990, 1991, 1993–2002, 2004).
- Selected as driver of the year for all of American motor racing in 1996 by a national panel of motorsports journalists, the first drag racer ever so honored.
- Won 13 races, appeared in 16 final rounds, and won 65 elimination rounds en route to the 1996 championship. All are NHRA single season records.
- Was named to the Auto Racing All-America Team, selected by members of the American Auto Racing Writers and Broadcasters Association, a record 10-straight years (1993–2002) and 12 times overall.
- Current NHRA national record holder for quarter-mile time (4.665 seconds) and speed (333.58 miles per hour).
- Quickest in NHRA Funny Car history at 4.665 and first Funny Car driver to break the 4.90, 4.80, and 4.70 second barriers.

JOHN FORCE RACE STATISTICS

Car: Castrol GTX® Start-Up Ford Mustang Funny Car
Residence: Yorba Linda, California
Birth date: May 4, 1949

NHRA POWERᴀᴅᴇ SERIES SUMMARY

Year	Starts	Final Rounds	Wins	No. 1 Qualifier	Low ET	Top Speed	Win-Loss Record	Points Poss.
1978	1	0	0	0	0	0	0-1	23rd
1979	6	2	0	0	0	1	8-6	8th
1980	4	0	0	0	0	1	1-4	26th
1981	3	0	0	0	0	0	2-3	16th
1982	2	0	0	0	0	0	3-2	20th
1983	10	2	0	0	0	1	12-10	4th
1984	8	0	0	0	0	0	5-8	13th
1985	12	1	0	0	0	1	5-12	8th
With Team Castrol								
1986	14	3	0	1	1	2	16-14	4th
1987	13	5	1	2	2	1	21-12	4th
1988	16	4	3	5	2	2	28-13	3rd
1989	19	2	1	1	0	1	21-18	6th
1990	19	7	7	10	6	1	45-12	**Champion**
1991	18	10	5	2	1	0	48-13	**Champion**
1992	18	8	4	8	5	4	39-14	2nd
1993	18	13	11	7	7	6	56-7	**Champion**
1994	18	11	10	12	13	6	50-8	**Champion**
1995	19	11	6	9	9	6	50-13	**Champion**

Year	Starts	Final Rounds	Wins	No. 1 Qualifier	Low ET	Top Speed	Win-Loss Record	Points Poss.
1996	19	16**	13**	13**	14	6	65-6**	**Champion**
1997	22	10	6	6	7	5	54-16	**Champion**
1998	22	9	3	4	4	10	44-19	**Champion**
1999	22	13	11	9	16**	12	61-11	**Champion**
2000	23	13	11	11	10	15**	58-12	**Champion**
2001	24	13	6	6	6	6	55-18	**Champion**
2002	23	10	8	6	6	3	48-15	**Champion**
2003	23	5	3	5	4	3	33-20	3rd
2004	23	12	5	7	5	6	53-18	**Champion**
2005	22	7	5	1	2	1	34-17	3rd
Totals	440	187*	119*	125**	120**	99*	925-322	

* NHRA POWERade Series record
** Funny Car division record

SOURCES

Interviews with: John McNichols, Susan Wade, Larry Sutton, Steve Querico, Joe Sherk, Bill Schultz, Don Prudhomme, Mike Dunn, Henry Velasco, Tony Pedregon, Wally Parks, Cruz Pedregon, Paul Kelly, Al Hofmann, Bill Bader, Vince Neal, John Sturbin, Dave McClelland, and Whit Bazemore.

Archival research and quotes from: *The Arizona Republic, Asbury Park Press, The Dallas Morning News, Ft. Worth Star-Telegram, Las Vegas Sun, Las Vegas Review-Journal, Los Angeles Times, New York Daily News, St. Petersburg Times, Seattle Post-Intelligencer, The Seattle Times, USA Today; Car Craft, Hot Rod, National Dragster, National Speed Sport News, Performance Trends, Winston Drag Racing Review; Brute Force;* NHRA Media Guides, CNN/SI.com, Competitionplus.com, Draglist.com, Dragracecentral.com, Dragracingonline.com, JohnForce.com, Johniesbroiler.com, RacingOne.com, NHRA.com; Team Force press releases.

INDEX